SIDE by SIDE
BILINGUAL BOOKS

Stories from Spain

Historias de España

Genevieve Barlow
William N. Stivers

PASSPORT BOOKS
NTC/Contemporary Publishing Group

Library of Congress Cataloging-in-Publication Data

Barlow, Genevieve.
    Stories from Spain – Historias de España / Genevieve Barlow and
William N. Stivers.
       p.   cm. — (Legends of—) (Side by side bilingual books)
    Engish and Spanish
    ISBN 0-8442-0499-4
    1. Spanish language—Readers—Legends.   2. Legends—Spain.
3.Spanish language—Textbooks for foreign speakers—English.   I.
Stivers, William N.   II. Title.   III. Title: Historias de España.   IV.
Series.   V. Series: Side by side bilingual books.
PC4127.L4B37   1999
468.6'421—dc21   99-10382
                                             CIP

Cover design by Nick Panos
Illustrated by George Armstrong and Jeff Stern

Special thanks to Dr. Phillip Thomason for his collaboration on "The Mysterious
Drawer" ("El cajón misterioso").

Published by Passport Books
A division of NTC/Contemporary Publishing Group, Inc.
4255 West Touhy Avenue, Lincolnwood (Chicago), Illinois 60712-1975 U.S.A.
Copyright © 1998 by NTC/Contemporary Publishing Group, Inc.
Printed in the United States of America
International Standard Book Number: 0-8442-0499-4
      02 03 04 05   20 19 18 17 16 15 14 13 12 11 10 9 8 7 6 5

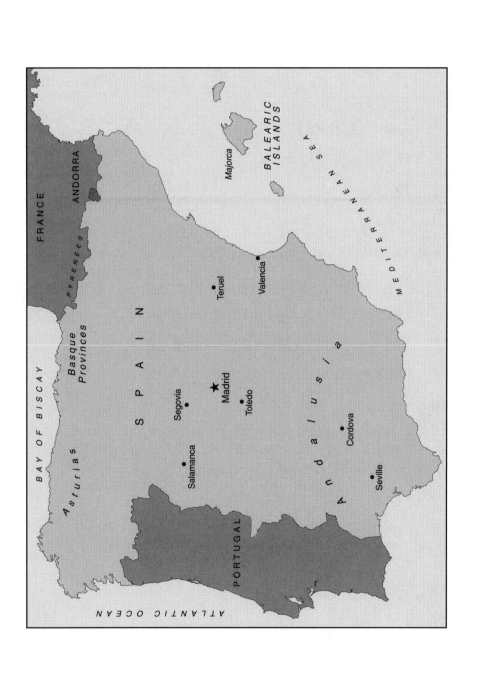

Contents

Contenido

Preface

SIDE BY SIDE BILINGUAL BOOKS introduce readers to engaging stories in a bilingual format, in which both versions of the text appear side by side on facing pages.

Stories from Spain/Historias de España explores the rich cultural and historical heritage of Spain. The eighteen legends are in chronological order and cover a period of more than a thousand years. We start with a legend that precedes the conquest by the Moors in the eighth century, and we conclude with a story that takes place at the end of the eighteenth century. The legends occur throughout Spain's geography: from the Basque Country in the north to Andalusia in the south, and from the austere land of Castile to the lush vegetation of Valencia along the Mediterranean coast.

The legends are presented in accessible language in both English and Spanish so readers may gain valuable reading skills in their new language while at the same time enjoying the support of their native language. Comprehension may be checked in either language by comparing the two versions of the story, or by referring to the bilingual vocabulary list at the end of the book.

It is our hope that readers will enjoy these captivating tales as they explore Spain's rich legacy.

Prólogo

SIDE BY SIDE BILINGUAL BOOKS ofrece a los lectores unas simpáticas historias bilingües, en las cuales las dos versiones del cuento aparecen lado a lado en páginas opuestas.

Stories from Spain/Historias de España explora la riqueza histórica y cultural de España. Las dieciocho leyendas están en orden cronológico y cubren un período de más de mil años. Empezamos con una leyenda que precede la época de la conquista de los moros en el siglo VIII y terminamos con una historia que tiene lugar a fines del siglo XVIII. Las leyendas transcurren a lo largo de la geografía de España: desde el País Vasco en el norte hasta Andalucía en el sur, y desde la austera tierra de Castilla hasta el paisaje exuberante de Valencia en la costa mediterránea.

Hemos publicado las leyendas de forma fácilmente comprensible en inglés y español para que los lectores puedan mejorar su habilidad para leer en su nuevo idioma, mientras siguen gozando del apoyo de su idioma materno. Es posible comprobar el grado de entendimiento comparando las dos versiones de la historia, y por medio de la lista bilingüe de vocabulario al final del libro.

Es nuestro deseo que los lectores disfruten de estas historias encantadoras mientras exploran la riqueza cultural que es España.

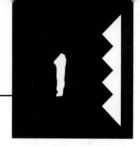

Lemor of Ireland

In northern Spain, there are three Basque provinces: Guipúzcoa, Biscay, and Álava. Their inhabitants are believed to be descendants of ancient peoples who once lived in France and Spain. The Basque[1] language is difficult to learn because it is unlike any other language. The Basques are industrious, independent, humble, and brave. One of their favorite pastimes is playing jai alai.[2] In addition, sailors from these provinces have the reputation of being the best in all of Spain.

Lémor de Irlanda

En el norte de España se encuentran tres provincias vascongadas: Guipúzcoa, Vizcaya y Álava. Se cree que sus habitantes son descendientes de pueblos muy antiguos que una vez vivieron en Francia y España. La lengua vasca[1] es difícil de aprender; no se parece a ninguna otra lengua. Los vascos son gente industriosa, independiente, sencilla y valiente. Uno de sus juegos favoritos es el jai alai.[2] Se dice también que los marineros de estas provincias son los mejores de España.

---

[1]It is also known as *Euskarian*.
[2]Game played by two or four players with a long curved basket strapped to the wrist and a ball that is bounced off a wall.

[1]También conocida como *euskera*.
[2]Juego de pelota en que participan dos o cuatro jugadores. Se juega en una cancha con una cesta alargada amarrada a la muñeca del jugador y con una pelota que se hace rebotar en un frontón.

Many years ago, there was a king in Ireland named Morna. All the people loved the king and his two sons, Lemor and Armin, who were good and noble young men.

One morning, the king and the princes, accompanied by many servants, set out to hunt wild boars that abounded in the nearby forest. The king and some of his servants entered the forest from one side; the princes and other servants entered by the other side. Soon, Lemor, the older son, shouted, "There goes a wild boar, near those tall oaks!"

Lemor's arrow immediately went flying in that direction. He, Armin, and the servants went in search of the animal. But the arrow had not struck a wild boar. As they drew near the tall oaks, they heard a cry of agony and they saw the king lying on the ground. The arrow had struck King Morna's chest. Moments later, he died. This tragedy caused great sorrow among the people. Lemor was inconsolable.

When everyone had returned to the castle, the elderly chiefs held a meeting. After long hours of discussion, they called for Lemor, the heir to the throne, and told him, "Lemor, although you are not to blame, it was your arrow that killed your beloved father. For that reason, you cannot be our king. Armin, your younger brother, will take your place. Tomorrow you will leave Ireland in a small boat with two of your servants. May a good wind accompany you! And may heaven guide you!"

The following morning, very early, the prince and his servants set sail. Sad and weary, they spent many days at sea.

Finally, Lemor saw land. Upon arriving, he and his servants were deeply impressed. They saw that the land was as green and beautiful as Ireland.

*H*ace muchos años, vivió en Irlanda un buen rey llamado Morna. Todo el pueblo amaba al rey y a sus dos hijos, Lémor y Armín, jóvenes nobles y buenos.

Una mañana, el rey y los príncipes, acompañados de muchos de sus criados, salieron a cazar jabalíes, los cuales abundaban en el bosque cercano. El rey y algunos de los criados entraron por un lado del bosque y los príncipes y otros criados por otro. De pronto Lémor, el hijo mayor, gritó:

—Ahí va un jabalí, cerca de esos altos robles.

En seguida, la flecha de Lémor fue volando en aquella dirección. Él, Armín y los criados fueron en busca del animal. Pero la flecha no dio en el jabalí. Al acercarse a los robles, oyeron un grito de agonía y vieron al rey tendido en el suelo. La flecha estaba hundida en el pecho del rey Morna. Momentos después, murió el rey y todos lloraron tristemente la tragedia. Lémor estaba desconsolado.

Al volver todos al castillo, se reunieron los jefes ancianos. Después de hablar largas horas, llamaron a Lémor, el heredero al trono, y le dijeron:

—Lémor, aunque usted no tiene culpa, ha sido su flecha la que ha matado a su querido padre. Por eso, usted no podrá ser nuestro rey. Armín, su hermano menor, ocupará su lugar. Y mañana usted con dos de sus criados, saldrán de Irlanda en un pequeño barco. ¡Que buen viento le acompañe y que el Cielo le guíe!

A la mañana siguiente muy temprano, el príncipe y sus criados partieron. Tristes y fatigados, pasaron muchos días en el mar.

Al fin, Lémor vio tierra. Al llegar él y sus criados, quedaron muy impresionados. Vieron que la tierra era tan verde y hermosa como en Irlanda.

Fortunately, they had arrived in the Basque country, home of kind and generous people. On seeing the strangers on the beach, men and women left their work and ran to offer them help. After learning who they were, Lekobide, the leader, offered them a second country. Each one was taken to a hospitable family, where he could live as a member of that family. Because Lemor was a prince, he was invited to be the guest of the leader and his family.

Everyone was happy with his new family, especially Lemor. He had fallen in love with the beautiful daughter of the leader and, with his permission, he wanted to marry her.

The day of the wedding, Lekobide fell seriously ill. To make matters worse, that same day the sentinels notified them that the Asturians,[2] their enemies from the west, were advancing rapidly, intent on waging war.

"What are we going to do without Lekobide?" everyone shouted. The Basque soldiers were brave, but they needed a good leader.

From his bed, Lekobide told them, "Many years have passed since the last wars and now I am old and sick. I cannot continue as your leader. But I have a solution. Lemor, who is now my son-in-law, has noble blood in his veins. He will be your leader."

At first Lemor did not want to accept, but everyone insisted.

"Yes, you are now our leader," said the people.

And Lemor, taking leave of his new wife, took his place at the head of the soldiers, and all of them started up the mountain to fight against the Asturian troops. Soon the Basques, led by Lemor, conquered the Asturians.

The Basque women went to receive the victorious soldiers with open arms. Lemor's wife, through tears of happiness, shouted with all of the women, "God bless our new leader!"

It is said that for many years the descendants of Lemor and Lekobide's daughter continued being leaders, worthy representatives of two noble races.

---

[2]People of Asturias in north central Spain.

Afortunadamente, habían llegado ellos a la tierra de los vascos, gente amable y generosa. Al ver a los extranjeros en la playa, hombres y mujeres abandonaron sus labores y corrieron a ofrecerles ayuda. Lekobide, el caudillo, al enterarse de quiénes eran, les ofreció una segunda patria. Cada uno de los viajeros fue llevado a casa de gentes hospitalarias donde podía vivir como miembro de la familia. Lémor, por ser príncipe, fue invitado a ser huésped del caudillo y su familia.

Todos estaban contentos con sus nuevas familias, especialmente Lémor. El príncipe se había enamorado de la hermosa hija del caudillo y, con autorización de éste, quería casarse con ella.

El día de la boda, Lekobide cayó gravemente enfermo. Y para empeorar las cosas, aquel día también los centinelas avisaron que los asturianos, sus enemigos del oeste, venían en son de guerra avanzando rápidamente.

—¿Qué vamos a hacer sin Lekobide? —gritaron todos. Eran valientes los soldados vascos, pero necesitaban un buen caudillo.

Desde la cama, Lekobide les dijo:

—Han pasado muchos años desde las últimas guerras y ahora estoy enfermo y viejo. No puedo seguir siendo su caudillo. Pero tengo la solución. Lémor, quien ahora es mi yerno, lleva sangre noble en sus venas: él será su caudillo.

Al principio, Lémor no quiso aceptar, pero todos insistieron.

—Sí, usted será ahora nuestro caudillo —dijeron todos.

Y Lémor, despidiéndose de su nueva esposa, se puso a la cabeza de los soldados y todos se lanzaron montaña arriba contra las tropas de los asturianos. Muy pronto los vascos, guiados por Lémor, vencieron a los asturianos.

Las mujeres fueron a recibir con brazos abiertos a los victoriosos soldados. La esposa de Lémor, llorando de felicidad, gritó con todas:

—¡Que Dios bendiga a nuestro nuevo caudillo!

Se dice que, por muchos años, los descendientes de Lémor y la hija de Lekobide siguieron siendo caudillos, dignos representantes de dos nobles razas.

2

The Gypsy's Prophecy

At the beginning of the eighth century, the Moors from the north of Africa invaded Spain. In only seven years, they were able to dominate almost the whole peninsula except for the northern mountains and some areas in the Pyrenees.[1] In the part that is now Asturias lived the noble Visigoth,[2] Don Pelayo, and his compatriots. This legend tells of a battle between the Visigoths and the Moors in the year 718.

La profecía de la gitana

A principios del siglo VIII, los moros del norte de África invadieron España. En tan sólo siete años llegaron a dominar casi toda la península, excepto las montañas del norte y algunas regiones de los Pirineos.[1] En la parte que hoy se llama Asturias, vivieron el noble visigodo[2] don Pelayo y sus compatriotas. Esta leyenda trata de una batalla que libraron los visigodos contra los moros en el año 718.

---

[1] Mountains along the French-Spanish border.
[2] One of the Germanic tribes that invaded Spain after the fall of the Roman Empire.

[1] Cadena montañosa situada en el límite entre Francia y España.
[2] Los visigodos fueron una de las tribus germánicas que invadieron España tras la caída del Imperio Romano.

Abd al-Aziz, a Moorish prince, was very sad, and with good reason. He had just lost his first battle in the long and bloody war against Don Pelayo and his soldiers. All the Moorish soldiers who had not died in battle were taken prisoners by Don Pelayo. Only the prince and his servant had been able to escape the hands of the enemy. Now they were fleeing toward the south in the direction of a tall mountain. There they hoped to spend the night.

It was late and the two Moors were exhausted, hungry, and thirsty, but they did not dare seek help. They were afraid of being discovered by the enemy.

After walking until nightfall, they arrived at the tall mountain where they discovered a large cave.

"Let's hide here," said the servant. "Perhaps our enemies won't discover us."

"Very well," answered Abd al-Aziz. "I am sure that Allah[3] will protect us, especially if there is a spider around here."

The servant looked with surprise at the prince, thinking that the poor fellow had surely lost his mind due to the many battles.

"Don't worry, my friend, I am not insane. I simply happen to remember what a gypsy woman told me in Granada."[4]

"What did the gypsy tell you?" the servant asked.

"She told me that someday a spider is going to save my life. For that reason, I have not hurt or killed a spider since that day. What do you think? Am I doing the right thing?"

But the faithful servant did not answer. He fell asleep on the ground on a bed of dry leaves. The prince also lay down and fell asleep.

The following morning, the two men awoke to loud voices and footsteps near their hiding place. A group of armed men was nearing the entrance of the cave.

"The Visigoths!" whispered the servant to his master.

"Let's look here!" one of the group shouted from outside, getting ready to enter.

---

[3]The God of Islam.
[4]City in the southern region of Andalusia, famous for its palace of La Alhambra.

Abd al-Aziz, noble príncipe moro, estaba muy triste, y con razón. Él acababa de perder su primera batalla del largo y sangriento conflicto con don Pelayo y sus soldados. Todos los soldados moros que no murieron en la batalla fueron hechos prisioneros por don Pelayo. Sólo el príncipe y su criado habían podido escaparse de las manos del enemigo. Ahora ellos huían hacia el sur en dirección a una alta montaña. Allí querían pasar la noche.

Era tarde y los dos moros estaban casi muertos de la fatiga. Además, tenían hambre y sed; pero no se atrevían a buscar ayuda. Tenían miedo de ser descubiertos por el enemigo.

Después de caminar hasta que fue de noche, llegaron a la alta montaña donde descubrieron una cueva inmensa.

—Vamos a escondernos aquí —dijo el criado—. Tal vez aquí nuestros enemigos no nos hallarán.

—Muy bien —respondió Abd al-Aziz—. Estoy seguro de que Alá[3] va a protegernos, especialmente si hay una araña aquí.

El criado miró con sorpresa al príncipe, creyendo que el pobre estaba loco debido a las muchas batallas.

—No se preocupe, amigo. No estoy loco. Es que todavía recuerdo bien lo que me dijo una gitana en Granada.

—¿Y qué le dijo esa gitana? —preguntó el criado.

—Me dijo: "Algún día una araña te va a salvar la vida". Por eso desde aquel momento nunca he herido o matado una araña. ¿Qué cree usted? ¿Hago bien?

Pero el fiel criado no dijo nada. Se durmió en el suelo sobre una cama de hojas secas. El príncipe también se acostó y se durmió.

A la mañana siguiente, los dos hombres se despertaron al oír fuertes voces y pasos cerca de su escondite. Un grupo de hombres armados se acercaba a la entrada de la cueva.

—¡Los visigodos! —dijo el criado a su señor en voz baja.

—Vamos a buscar aquí —gritó uno del grupo de afuera, preparándose para entrar.

---

[3]Dios de los mahometanos.

"It's useless," another answered. "No one has entered there!"

"How do you know?"

"Can't you see? Look at the large spiderweb that is spun from one side to the other at the entrance of the cave. No one could have entered!"

Everyone looked at the entrance and they saw that, indeed, a spiderweb covered the whole entrance of the cave.

"We must notify Don Pelayo that the Moorish prince and his servant are nowhere to be found," said one of the Visigoths. "They have managed to escape."

Inside the cave, the prince and his servant looked at each other in awe. It seemed a miracle that they had escaped detection. During the night, a spider had woven that life-saving curtain. They owed their lives to a spider.

"It's the providential spider the gypsy spoke about," said the prince. "Without it, we would surely be in the hands of the enemy. Thank you, blessed spider."

—Es inútil —contestó otro—. ¡Nadie ha entrado allí!

—¿Cómo lo sabe usted?

—Hombre, ¿no tiene usted ojos? ¿No ve en la entrada de la cueva una gran telaraña que la cubre de un lado a otro? ¿Por dónde entraría uno?

Todos miraron la entrada y vieron que había, en efecto, una telaraña que cubría la entrada de la cueva.

—Tendremos que notificar a don Pelayo que el príncipe y su criado no aparecen por ninguna parte —dijo uno de los visigodos—. Han logrado escabullirse.

Dentro de la cueva, el príncipe y su criado se miraron admirados. Les pareció un milagro. Durante la noche, una araña había construido aquella cortina salvadora y los dos le debían su vida a esa araña.

—Es la araña providencial de que habló la gitana —dijo el príncipe—. Sin ella estaríamos a estas horas en poder del enemigo. ¡Gracias, bendita araña!

3

The Ransom

During the Wars of Reconquest[1] when the Spanish fought to oust the Moors, many of the noblemen distinguished themselves by their brave deeds. But, as always, there were some traitors. This legend describes the treason of Don Pedro and the bravery of Don Artal de Luna and his daughter, Doña Jimena.

El rescate

Durante las guerras de Reconquista[1] en que los españoles lucharon para expulsar a los moros de España, muchos señores nobles se distinguieron por sus valerosos hechos. Pero, como siempre, hubo también traidores. Esta leyenda narra la traición de don Pedro y habla del valor de don Artal de Luna y su hija, doña Jimena.

---

[1]The Reconquest began in the eighth century and ended in 1492 after the fall of Granada.

[1]La Reconquista de España se inició en el siglo VIII y terminó con la toma de Granada en 1492 por los Reyes Católicos Fernando e Isabel.

Around the year 1232, when Don Jaime I the Conqueror was king of Aragón,[2] many brave noblemen gave their services to the king and the Wars of Reconquest. One of the bravest was Don Artal de Luna. He was one of the most faithful and devoted. On the other hand, Don Pedro Ahones, seizing the opportunity, betrayed the king and fought on the side of the Moors.

Discovering this betrayal, Don Artal swore vengeance and wanted to punish Don Pedro. Even though Don Artal's men were outnumbered by those of Don Pedro, Don Artal did not hesitate. The two noblemen and their soldiers fought. Don Pedro was able to defeat Don Artal and make him his prisoner.

It was customary at the time to grant the prisoners an opportunity to pay a ransom for their freedom.

"Don Pedro," Don Artal said, "set the price of the ransom, and I shall pay it to you."

"But Don Artal," responded Don Pedro, "I have already sent messengers to your castle with the price of the ransom. I trust that your daughter will pay it."

Don Artal suspected his daughter might be in danger, but he could do nothing.

When Doña Jimena, Don Artal's daughter, saw the messengers approaching the castle, she knew her father was in danger. One of the messengers entered the palace and gave a parchment to Doña Jimena. She read:

My lady, Doña Jimena,

Your father has been defeated and is now my prisoner.

I ask your hand in exchange for his life and liberty.

Your constant admirer

---

[2]One of the many kingdoms in which Spain was divided before its unification under King Ferdinand and Queen Isabella.

Alrededor del año 1232, cuando don Jaime I el Conquistador era rey de Aragón,[2] hubo señores muy valientes que prestaron sus servicios en favor del rey y las guerras de Reconquista. Uno de los más valientes fue don Artal de Luna. Era él de los más fieles y devotos. En cambio, don Pedro Ahones, al ver la primera oportunidad, traicionó al rey y se puso del lado de los moros.

Al darse cuenta de esta traición, don Artal juró venganza y decidió castigar a don Pedro. Aunque las fuerzas de don Artal eran inferiores en número a las de don Pedro, don Artal no vaciló. Los dos nobles y sus soldados pelearon. Don Pedro venció a don Artal y lo tomó prisionero.

Era costumbre en ese tiempo dar oportunidad a los prisioneros de pagar un rescate por su libertad.

—Don Pedro —dijo don Artal—, fije la cantidad del rescate y se la pagaré.

—Pero, don Artal —respondió don Pedro—, ya he enviado mensajeros a su castillo con el precio del rescate. Confío que su hija lo pagará.

Don Artal sospechó peligro para su hija, pero no pudo hacer nada.

Cuando doña Jimena, la hija de don Artal, vio a los mensajeros acercarse al castillo, supo que su padre estaba en peligro. Uno de los mensajeros entró en el palacio y le dio a doña Jimena un pergamino. Ella lo leyó:

Señora mía, doña Jimena:

Su padre ha sido vencido y es ahora mi prisionero. Le pido a usted su mano a cambio de la vida y libertad de su padre.

Su constante admirador

---

[2] Uno de los reinos en que se encontraba dividida España antes de su unificación bajo la corona de los Reyes Católicos.

She did not move a muscle in her face. She hesitated a moment and then said to the messenger, "I accept the price that Don Pedro has set for the life and liberty of my father. But since I don't trust him, I want to see my father here first and then, on my word of honor, his request will be granted."

The messenger left the castle and returned to Don Pedro's encampment with Doña Jimena's words. When Don Pedro heard the answer, he felt a diabolic pleasure because everything had been so very easy.

The following day, accompanied by the same messenger, Don Artal was sent to his castle. From far away, he could see his daughter in one of the windows of the tower. Don Artal dismissed the messenger and entered the castle. At that moment, through one of the back doors, a mysterious knight left the castle at full gallop.

The knight finally arrived at Don Pedro's camp. He immediately asked to speak with Don Pedro. He had a small box in one hand and a parchment in the other. Surprised, Don Pedro accepted the parchment and began to read:

Don Pedro,

You have kept your word by giving my father his liberty. His life is worth more than my hand. I now send it to you, but you shall never have my heart.

Doña Jimena

Confused, Don Pedro opened the box. Wrapped in silk lay a woman's recently cut hand, still bleeding.

Ella no movió ni un músculo de la cara. Esperó un momento y luego le dijo al mensajero:

—Acepto el precio que don Pedro pide por la vida y libertad de mi padre. Pero como no me fío de él, deseo ver a mi padre aquí primero y luego, por mi honor, su petición será cumplida.

El mensajero salió del castillo y volvió al campamento de don Pedro con las palabras de doña Jimena. Cuando don Pedro oyó la respuesta, sintió un gozo diabólico, porque todo había sido muy fácil.

Al día siguiente, acompañado del mismo mensajero, don Artal fue enviado a su castillo. De lejos podía ver a su hija en una de las ventanas de la torre. Don Artal despidió al mensajero y entró en el castillo. En ese momento, por una puerta de atrás, salió un misterioso caballero a todo galope.

El caballero llegó finalmente al campamento de don Pedro y pidió hablar con él. Llevaba un pequeño cofre en una mano y un pergamino en la otra. Don Pedro, sorprendido, aceptó el pergamino y comenzó a leer:

Don Pedro:

Usted ha cumplido su palabra al darle a mi padre su libertad. La vida de él vale más que mi mano. Se la mando entonces, pero nunca tendrá usted mi corazón.

Doña Jimena

Don Pedro, confuso, abrió el cofre. Envuelta en sedas estaba una mano de mujer recién cortada y todavía sangrienta.

The Lovers of Teruel

The Village of Teruel, today noted for its fine collection of Mudejar[1] towers and churches, is located due east of Madrid in Aragón on the road from Zaragoza to Valencia. This road had been an important route during the Middle Ages.

The legend of "the lovers" is very well known and is frequently retold. It was immortalized in Hartzenbusch's romantic drama "Los amantes de Teruel." According to the introduction of the same play by Lewis E. Brett, the origin and authenticity of the legend are greatly disputed. There are those, however, who claim that the exact year of the tragedy is 1217, that the

Continued on p. 20

Los amantes de Teruel

La ciudad de Teruel, conocida hoy por su fina colección de torres e iglesias de estilo mudéjar,[1] se encuentra en Aragón, al este de Madrid, sobre la carretera que va de Zaragoza a Valencia. Esta carretera fue una ruta importante durante la Edad Media.

La leyenda de los amantes es muy conocida y se relata con frecuencia. Fue inmortalizada en la obra romántica de Hartzenbusch, *Los amantes de Teruel*. Según la introducción de la misma obra por Brett, el origen y la autenticidad de la leyenda son muy disputados. Hay aquéllos, sin embargo, que aseguran que la tra-

Continued on p. 21

---

[1]Architectural style that flourished in Spain from the thirteenth to the sixteenth century, characterized by the fusion of Romanesque, Gothic, and Arabic art elements.

[1]Estilo arquitectónico en el que se combinan elementos románicos, góticos y árabes. Floreció en España en los siglos XIII a XVI.

two lovers lived on Ricoshombres Street, and that their remains are on display in the church of San Pedro.[2] In any case, the legend is alive and well in our day.

*I*n the city of Teruel, in the province of Aragón, lived Diego Marcilla and Isabel de Segura. Since childhood, they were the best of friends. They always used to play and were seen together. They were inseparable. He was from a poor family, but she belonged to one of the principal families of the area. As the years went by, their friendship turned into love. Isabel was a beautiful young lady, and Diego, a handsome fellow who dreamed of making a name for himself as a soldier.

"You'll see," he said to Isabel, "I'll go off to war with the King's troops. I'll fight bravely and try to earn fame and wealth. I'll march with the other soldiers and you'll see me off, waving the lace handkerchief that I gave you."

All this pleased Isabel, but destiny had reserved something else for them. Isabel's cousin, Elena, while visiting Isabel, met Diego and instantly fell madly in love with him. From that moment on Elena looked for ways to separate Diego and Isabel so that she could marry him.

In the same city there lived a young noble named Fernando de Gamboa. Elena wrote a love note to him and signed Isabel's name. Fernando had planned to leave the city, but on receiving the note, he decided to stay and pursue, if it were possible, the intention of the note. For several days he walked in front of Isabel's house, but Isabel never came out. He thought that she was just being shy.

Meanwhile, Fernando spoke to Isabel's parents indicating that he would like to marry Isabel. Isabel's parents, realizing that she was of marrying age and despite the love that she had for Diego, thought that she should be given to Fernando. Diego was poor and Fernando was rich.

[2]Lewis E. Brett, ed., *Nineteenth Century Spanish Plays.* (New York: Appleton-Century-Crofts, Inc., 1935), p. 123.

gedia tuvo lugar en 1217, que los amantes vivieron en la calle de los Ricoshombres y que sus restos reposan en la iglesia de San Pedro. Pero, en todo caso, la leyenda sigue viva aún hoy.

En la ciudad de Teruel, provincia de Aragón, vivieron Diego Marcilla e Isabel de Segura. Desde niños fueron muy amigos. Siempre jugaban y estaban juntos. Eran inseparables. Él era de familia pobre, pero ella pertenecía a una familia principal de la comarca. Al pasar los años, la amistad se volvió en amor. Isabel era ya una linda señorita y Diego un galán que soñaba con llegar a ser un famoso soldado.

—Verás —le dijo a Isabel—, partiré a la guerra con las tropas del rey. Pelearé con valor y trataré de ganar fama y riqueza. Me marcharé con los otros soldados y tú me despedirás con el pañuelo de encaje que te regalé.

Todo esto le dio mucho gusto a Isabel, pero el destino les había reservado algo inesperado. Una prima de Isabel, Elena, cuando visitaba a su prima, conoció a Diego y al instante se enamoró locamente de él. Desde aquel momento Elena buscó cómo separar a Diego de Isabel para que ella pudiera casarse con él.

En la misma ciudad vivía un joven noble llamado Fernando de Gamboa. Elena le escribió una nota amorosa y firmó el nombre de Isabel. Fernando tenía pensado salir de la ciudad; pero al recibir esta nota, decidió quedarse y corresponder, si fuera posible, el ánimo de la nota. Durante varios días él rondó por la casa de Isabel, pero Isabel nunca apareció. Él pensaba que era tímida.

Mientras tanto, Fernando habló con los padres de Isabel informándoles que quería casarse con ella. Los padres, sabiendo que ella estaba en edad de casarse y a pesar del amor que ella tenía por Diego, pensaron que ella debía casarse con Fernando. Diego era pobre y Fernando era rico.

Because of the notes Fernando had received, supposedly from Isabel, he thought he would have no difficulty with her. In speaking with Isabel's parents, he reminded them of his noble family and his great wealth.

Diego also spoke with her parents and said, "I am not rich, nor of the nobility, but since I was a child I have been in your home, and you know that I love Isabel. I will make a good husband for her."

The parents decided, however, that Fernando was the better choice since he was a nobleman and wealthy. Saddened, Diego begged the parents to wait until he could gain honor and fame as a soldier before they allowed the marriage with Fernando. The parents decided to grant his request and said that they would wait three years and three days. The father said, "If you return within the given time with honor and wealth, or if you are famous, Isabel will be yours. But we shall not wait even one hour more than what has been agreed."

Diego accepted this gladly and explained everything to Isabel. He was confident that he would succeed, but Isabel was not as certain.

The wars were many and varied. Sometimes, with just a few men, the troops would go on dangerous expeditions.

They mainly fought the Moors. Diego fought with such valor that he gained fame and fortune, and was even granted a title of nobility. Now he knew that he would be able to marry Isabel!

Elena, however, did not give up on her intention to marry Diego. She went to Isabel's father and told him that she had heard from a good source that Diego had died heroically on the battlefield. Isabel's father then sadly told Isabel. Isabel suspected that this was not true. She remembered that Diego had told her that he would return before the set time, so she begged her father to wait until the very last moment.

The time finally expired. Don Diego was not able to arrive within the given time and Isabel had to marry Fernando.

Debido a las notas que había recibido y suponiendo que eran de Isabel, Fernando creyó que no tendría ninguna dificultad con ella. Al hablar con los padres de Isabel, él les recordó que era de familia noble y de gran fortuna.

Diego también habló con los padres y les dijo:

—No soy rico ni noble, pero desde niño he visitado su casa y ustedes saben que yo amo a Isabel. Yo seré buen esposo para ella.

Los padres decidieron, sin embargo, que Fernando sería mejor esposo, ya que era noble y rico. Diego, entristecido, les rogó a los padres que esperaran hasta que él pudiera ganar buen nombre y fama de soldado antes de permitir el matrimonio con Fernando. Los padres le concedieron su petición y dijeron que esperarían tres años y tres días. El padre dijo:

—Si tú vienes dentro del plazo de tiempo fijado con honor y riquezas, o si eres famoso, Isabel será tuya. Pero no vamos a esperar ni una hora más de lo acordado.

Diego aceptó esto con gusto y le explicó todo a Isabel. Él estaba muy confiado de que podría lograr su propósito, pero Isabel no estaba tan segura.

Las guerras fueron muchas y variadas. A veces, con pocos soldados iban las tropas a peligrosas expediciones.

Pelearon principalmente contra los moros y fue tan valiente Diego que ganó fama y fortuna. Además, le otorgaron un título de nobleza. Ahora sabía que podía casarse con Isabel.

Elena, no obstante, no renunció a su intención de casarse con Diego. Ella fue al padre de Isabel y le dijo que había oído de buena fuente que Diego había muerto heroicamente en el campo de batalla. El padre luego fue y se lo dijo tristemente a Isabel. Isabel sospechaba que esto no era verdad. Se acordó de que Diego le había dicho que volvería antes del plazo fijado, y por eso le rogó al padre que esperara hasta el último momento.

Finalmente, se cumplió el plazo. Don Diego no pudo llegar a tiempo e Isabel tuvo que casarse con Fernando.

Two hours after the set time, Diego arrived as fast as he could, changing horses and galloping as fast as they would go. But he was too late. He went up to Isabel's room and saw that it was decorated for the new bride. He hid under the bed and waited for the newly married couple. When they arrived, he managed to find Isabel's hand. She, at once, recognized who it was. Isabel asked her new husband to go find some smelling salts. When he had left the room, Diego asked her why she had not waited. "I waited until the last moment," she said. "But now I am married before God and I cannot tarnish my honor by leaving with you."

Diego insisted and felt such sadness in his heart that he fell dead on the spot.

When Fernando returned, Isabel explained to him all that had happened, indicating that she was completely innocent. Fernando arranged to carry Diego's body to the doorway of his own house, where his parents found him the next morning.

Many people attended his funeral. Isabel was there too, dressed in black. She approached the coffin and gave Diego a passionate kiss. When Fernando saw what had happened, he tried to lift Isabel from the coffin, but on attempting to do this, he realized that she, too, had died.

Don Fernando then sadly said, "In life they were not united, but in death they shall be."

And true to what he said, they were buried together with great ceremony, and to this day all of Spain knows about the lovers of Teruel.

Dos horas después del plazo, llegó Diego tan pronto como pudo, cambiando caballos al galope. Pero llegó demasiado tarde. Subió al cuarto de Isabel y vio que estaba decorado para la boda. Se escondió debajo de la cama y esperó a los recién casados. Cuando éstos llegaron, Diego buscó la mano de Isabel. Ella inmediatamente reconoció de quién era. Isabel luego le pidió a su nuevo esposo que fuera en busca de sales. Cuando él salió del cuarto, Diego le preguntó por qué ella no había esperado. Ella dijo: —Yo esperé hasta el último momento. Pero ahora estoy casada delante de Dios y no puedo faltar a mi honor yéndome contigo ahora.

Diego insistió y sintió tanta tristeza de corazón que murió al instante.

Cuando Fernando volvió, Isabel le explicó lo que había pasado, jurándole que ella era inocente de todo. Fernando hizo los arreglos necesarios para que el cuerpo de Diego fuera llevado al portal de su propia casa, donde sus padres lo encontraron la mañana siguiente.

Mucha gente asistió al funeral. Isabel estuvo también, vestida de negro. Se acercó al ataúd y le dio a Diego un beso apasionado. Cuando Fernando vio lo que había pasado, fue a levantar a Isabel del ataúd; pero, al tratar de hacer esto, se dio cuenta de que ella también había muerto. Don Fernando luego dijo: —En vida no estuvieron unidos, pero en la muerte sí estarán.

Y era verdad lo que dijo. Fueron sepultados juntos con gran ceremonia y hasta la fecha es conocida en toda España la leyenda de los amantes de Teruel.

Aliatar's Horse

All the horses of today are believed to be descendants of Arabian horses. These horses are undoubtedly noble animals and faithful friends to their owners. This legend tells of a special horse named Loyal, and of his owner, Aliatar, a Moorish prince who lived near Cordova.[1]

El caballo de Aliatar

Se dice que todos los caballos que existen hoy en día son descendientes de los caballos árabes. No hay duda de que son muy nobles y fieles a sus dueños. Esta leyenda nos habla del caballo de Aliatar. Aliatar era un príncipe moro que vivía cerca de la ciudad de Córdoba.[1] Su caballo se llamaba Leal.

---

[1] Spanish city in the southern region of Andalusia, famous for its Moorish mosque—La mezquita de Córdoba.

[1] Ciudad de Andalucía (región situada al sur de la península), famosa por su Mezquita.

One afternoon, Don Pedro de Gómez, from the parapet of his castle, saw a man running rapidly toward him. The man appeared to be very agitated. When he arrived at the castle, Don Pedro asked, "What's happening? Why such urgency?"

"Sir," said the man breathlessly, "all the laborers have abandoned the fields because the Moors have invaded our land!"

"The Moors!" Don Pedro exclaimed. And without notifying anyone in the castle, he went to the stables, saddled his horse, and left for one of the nearest fields.

Ignoring the risk, Don Pedro went through a forest that was not far from the field. The Moors, in hiding, were waiting for him. At just the right moment they ambushed him and took him prisoner. These soldiers served the great prince, Aliatar.

When the Moors notified the great Aliatar that Don Pedro was held prisoner, Aliatar came to talk to him.

"Don Pedro, Don Pedro, why did you let yourself fall into my hands?"

"Tell me the price of the ransom, Don Aliatar, and my children will pay it," Don Pedro answered.

"I prefer your person to your money," Aliatar answered with a smile. "Now let's get out of this forest because it will soon begin to rain. First, Don Pedro, hand over your sword to one of my soldiers."

Don Pedro obeyed and everyone began the march. It started to rain heavily and the sky became very dark. In all the confusion, Don Pedro and Aliatar were left alone, way behind the others. In an instant, Don Pedro realized that he was in a position to save himself. Unexpectedly, he knocked Aliatar off his horse and disarmed him. The faithful horse, Loyal, did not leave his master's side. They got on their horses again, turned around, and continued in the opposite direction to avoid Aliatar's soldiers. After the two men came out of the forest, Don Pedro's men arrived, and Aliatar's Moorish soldiers, who were pursuing Aliatar and Don Pedro, fled.

"Now you are my prisoner," Don Pedro said to Aliatar. "I can see that you had escaped from us before because you had such a fine horse."

*U*na tarde, don Pedro de Gómez, estando en el parapeto de su castillo, vio la figura de un hombre que corría rápidamente hacia él. Venía muy aprisa y agitado y, al llegar al castillo, don Pedro le preguntó:

—¿Qué pasa? ¿Por qué tanta urgencia?

—Señor —dijo el hombre—, los labradores han abandonado los campos porque los moros nos han invadido.

—¡Los moros! —repitió don Pedro. Y sin avisar a nadie en el castillo, fue al establo, ensilló su caballo y salió para uno de los campos más cercanos.

Sin poner atención al riesgo, don Pedro pasó por un bosque no muy lejos del campo. Los moros lo esperaban escondidos y al momento apropiado lo sorprendieron y lo tomaron preso. Estos soldados servían al gran príncipe Aliatar.

Cuando Aliatar fue avisado de que don Pedro estaba prisionero, vino en seguida a hablar con él.

—Don Pedro, don Pedro, ¿por qué se dejó caer en mis manos?

—Dígame el precio de mi rescate, don Aliatar, y mis hijos se lo pagarán —respondió don Pedro.

—Prefiero su persona a su dinero —contestó Aliatar con una sonrisa—. Ahora vamos a salir de este bosque porque pronto va a comenzar a llover. Primero, don Pedro, entregue su espada a uno de mis soldados.

Don Pedro obedeció y todos se pusieron en camino. Comenzó a llover a cántaros y el cielo se oscureció totalmente. En medio de la confusión, don Pedro y Aliatar se quedaron solos y detrás de los otros. Al instante, comprendió don Pedro que se le presentaba una ocasión favorable para salvarse. En un momento inesperado, tumbó a Aliatar de su caballo y pronto le quitó sus armas. El fiel Leal no salió del lado de su amo. Montados otra vez en caballo, dieron la vuelta y siguieron en dirección opuesta para evadir a los soldados de Aliatar. Al salir los dos del bosque, los hombres de don Pedro llegaron y los soldados moros que perseguían a don Pedro y a Aliatar huyeron.

—Ahora es usted mi prisionero —dijo don Pedro a Aliatar—. Y veo que usted se nos había escapado antes porque tenía tan buen caballo.

"Yes," Aliatar commented, caressing his horse and whispering in his ear. "Nothing can compare to my horse."

Don Pedro was highly impressed. He knew that the Moors loved their horses very much and that Loyal, Aliatar's horse, was one of the best.

Don Pedro, in a moment of great compassion, said to Aliatar, "Don Aliatar, you and your horse are free to go."

The great Moor was moved by this and wanted to thank Don Pedro for granting him his liberty.

"Thank you, thank you a thousand times," Aliatar said, and in a gesture of gratitude added, "You have treated me with great respect and affection." He approached Don Pedro and embraced him. The two of them began to talk as if they were old friends.

"You captured me and even though I am free, you have made me your slave," Aliatar said.

"How?" Don Pedro asked.

"Because you are now my friend."

"I have treated you exactly as you deserve, Aliatar. You are one of the most noble of your race."

"I assure you that my soldiers will not invade your land again," said Aliatar.

Having said this, Aliatar took his faithful horse's bridle and presented it to Don Pedro.

"I present him to you as a gift, in honor of our friendship."

Don Pedro was deeply moved and said, "I offer you my horse in exchange."

Aliatar then mounted Don Pedro's horse and gave Loyal his last caress, exclaiming, "May Allah keep you." Then he galloped off.

Loyal stood still, following his master with sad eyes. His new master caressed him in vain. Loyal refused to eat. He refused to enter the stable. He kept looking down the path where his old master had disappeared.

Days passed. Loyal fell ill and died. They say that he died of sadness. Because of this we can say that loyalty is a quality that is not limited only to good people.

—Sí —comentó Aliatar, acariciando su caballo y hablándole en voz baja al oído—. No hay otro como Leal.

Quedó muy impresionado don Pedro. Él sabía muy bien que los moros querían mucho a sus caballos; y Leal, el caballo de Aliatar, era de los mejores.

Don Pedro, en un momento de gran compasión, le dijo a Aliatar:

—Don Aliatar, usted y su caballo ya están libres.

Conmovido, el gran moro quiso agradecerle a don Pedro por su libertad.

—Gracias, mil gracias —dijo Aliatar y luego con un gesto de agradecimiento añadió:

—Ustedes me han tratado con gran respeto y afecto—. Y se acercó a don Pedro y lo abrazó. Los dos comenzaron a hablar como viejos amigos.

—Usted me ha vencido, y aunque estoy libre, me ha hecho su esclavo —dijo Aliatar.

—¿Cómo? —preguntó don Pedro.

—Porque ahora es usted mi amigo.

—Sólo he hecho lo que usted merece, Aliatar. Usted es uno de los más nobles de su raza.

—Le aseguro que mis soldados no volverán a invadir su tierra —dijo Aliatar.

Y al decir esto, Aliatar cogió la brida de su fiel caballo, Leal, y se lo presentó a don Pedro.

—Se lo regalo a usted como recuerdo de nuestra amistad.

Don Pedro, conmovido, dijo:

—Y yo le ofrezco mi caballo a cambio.

Aliatar luego montó el caballo de don Pedro e hizo a Leal la última caricia, exclamando:

—¡Que Alá los guarde! —y se marchó al galope.

Leal permaneció inmóvil, siguiendo con la mirada triste a su amo. En vano su nuevo amo lo acarició. Leal no quiso comer. No quiso entrar al establo. Quedó mirando el camino por donde su viejo amo había desaparecido.

Pasaron días. Leal se enfermó y murió. Dicen que murió de tristeza. Así se puede ver que la lealtad es una cualidad que no se limita sólo a las buenas personas.

The Woman Warrior

Andalusia,[1] the southernmost region of the peninsula, is the most Moorish part of Spain as well as the source of many fantastic tales. The combination of Moorish elements with the Spanish imagination has produced the most intriguing legends. There are even some who positively state that the events in these stories actually took place. At times, the truth can be more fantastic than the imagination.

La mujer guerrera

Andalucía,[1] situada al sur de la península, es la región más morisca de España, así como la fuente de muchos cuentos fantásticos. Se dice que la combinación de elementos moriscos y la imaginación española ha producido las leyendas más interesantes de toda España. Y no son pocos los que afirman que estos sucesos sí han ocurrido en la vida real. La verdad es a veces más fantástica que lo imaginado.

---

[1]The name "Andalusia" comes from "Vandalusia," that is, the land of the Vandals. The Vandals, like the Visigoths, were one of the Germanic tribes that invaded Spain after the fall of the Roman Empire.

[1]El nombre "Andalucía" deriva de "Vandalucía", es decir, tierra de los vándalos. Los vándalos, al igual que los visigodos, fueron una de las tribus germánicas que invadieron España tras la caída del Imperio Romano.

*M*any, many years ago, there lived in Andalusia a count who had no son. However, his wife, the countess, had given him seven daughters.

The count was desperate because the king had just declared war against the Moors and had published this decree:

"Each noble must contribute one of his sons to fight in the war against the Moors."

"Don't worry, father," Catalina said. Catalina was the youngest and most beautiful of his daughters. "I shall dress as a man and I shall command the troops."

"But your hands are too white and delicate to be those of a warrior," protested the count.

"Very soon the sun will change their color and they will be tan."

"They will know by your shape that you are a woman, my daughter."

"I shall wear the armor in such a way that no one will notice, father."

Her father gave her a horse, a suit of armor, a lance, a helmet, a shield, and some mesh gloves.

Then the count presented her to the troops as his nephew, Don Martín of Aragón. In just a short while, she and the troops left for war.

Catalina was brave and fought hard in battle. But when she retired to her tent at night, she would cry uncontrollably at having seen so many wounded and dead men.

One day, there was a fierce battle. In the most difficult part of the skirmish, Catalina saw a nobleman at the head of his troops shouting a war cry. He threw himself like a bolt of lightning against a large number of Moors. But the nobleman had not seen that behind him a battalion of Moors was coming. At that moment Catalina and her soldiers went to his aid. She arrived at the nobleman's side just in time to see him fall wounded. She took him up in her arms.

The soldiers carried him to her tent. Catalina attentively cared for him. Fortunately, his wounds were not life-threatening, and he soon regained his strength. Catalina discovered that the wounded captain was the king's son.

*H*ace muchísimos años, vivía en Andalucía un conde que no tenía hijo varón. En cambio, su esposa, la condesa, le había dado siete hijas.

El pobre conde estaba muy afligido porque el rey acababa de declarar una guerra contra los moros y había publicado este edicto:

Cada noble tiene que contribuir al reino un hijo para la guerra contra los moros.

—No se preocupe, padre —dijo Catalina, la más joven y la más bonita de sus hijas—. Yo me vestiré de hombre y comandaré las tropas.

—Pero tus manos son muy blancas y delicadas para ser las de un guerrero —dijo el conde.

—Muy pronto el sol cambiará su color y estarán morenas.

—Notarán en tu forma que eres mujer, hija mía.

—Yo usaré la armadura de tal modo que nadie lo notará.

Entonces el padre le dio un caballo, una armadura, una lanza, un casco, un escudo y unos guantes de malla.

El conde luego la presentó a las tropas como su sobrino, don Martín de Aragón. En poco tiempo ella y las tropas salieron para la guerra.

Catalina era valiente y dura en la batalla. Pero cuando se acostaba en su tienda de noche, lloraba sin consuelo por haber visto a tantos hombres heridos y muertos.

Un día hubo una gran batalla. En la parte más difícil de la lucha, vio Catalina a un caballero a la cabeza de sus tropas, gritando:

—¡Santiago, cierra, Santiago! —Y se lanzaba como un relámpago sobre un grupo de moros. Pero el caballero no había visto que detrás de él venía un batallón de moros. En aquel momento, Catalina y sus soldados fueron a su ayuda. Ella llegó junto al caballero a tiempo de verlo caer herido y lo recogió en sus brazos.

Los soldados lo llevaron a su tienda. Catalina lo cuidó con mucha atención. Afortunadamente las heridas del caballero no eran mortales y pronto recobró la salud. Catalina descubrió que el capitán herido era el hijo del rey.

But the king's son was disturbed by Catalina's eyes and her soft feminine hands. For that reason, when he recovered he went to talk to his mother, the queen, and told her, "Dear mother, I am confused because it seems that the eyes and hands of Don Martín are not those of a man, but of a woman."

"You should invite Don Martín to go to the fair with you. If she is a woman, she will go to look at the dresses."

But Don Martín, being discreet, went to look at the weapons. Taking a dagger in her hands, she said, "What a marvelous dagger this is to fight against the Moors!"

Then the king's son went to his mother to tell her what had happened.

"How am I going to prove that Don Martín is a woman?"

"I know what you should do. You can invite Don Martín to bathe in the river with some of the soldiers."

When Don Martín received the invitation, she said that she could not accept. Her father was very ill and she had to go home immediately.

Don Martín received permission from the king to go home to her sick father. On taking her leave of the king, she said, "Good-bye, good king. I wish to confess now that for two years, a woman has served you. I did it because my father has no sons. And I did it very proudly. Long live the king!"

The king's son heard the conversation and, mounting his horse, ran after her. But Don Martín's horse arrived first at the count's palace.

The count was very happy. He knew that through his daughter, he had fulfilled his duty.

The prince, arriving at the gate of the castle, knocked and asked for Don Martín. Catalina came out to receive him. Realizing who she was, he fell in love with her instantly. He asked the count for her hand in marriage.

It is said that this couple lived happily for many years.

Pero el hijo del rey estaba turbado por los ojos de Catalina y sus suaves manos de mujer. Por eso, cuando se recuperó, fue a hablar con su madre, la reina, y le dijo:

—Querida madre, estoy turbado porque me parece que los ojos y las manos de don Martín no son de hombre, sino de mujer.

—Debes invitar a don Martín a acompañarte a la feria. Si es mujer, irá a mirar los vestidos.

Pero, don Martín, siendo discreto, fue a mirar las armas; y, tomando en la mano un puñal, dijo:

—¡Qué maravilloso puñal es éste para pelear contra los moros!

Luego el hijo del rey fue con su madre a contarle lo que había pasado.

—¿Cómo voy a hacer para probar que don Martín es mujer?

—Yo sé lo que debes hacer. Puedes invitar a don Martín a bañarse en el río con algunos de los soldados.

Cuando don Martín recibió la invitación, dijo que no podía aceptar. Su padre estaba muy enfermo y tenía que ir a su casa inmediatamente.

Don Martín recibió permiso del rey para volver a su casa para estar con su padre enfermo. Al despedirse, ella le dijo al rey:

—Adiós, buen Rey. Quiero confesar ahora que durante dos años le ha servido una mujer. Lo hice porque mi padre no tiene hijos. Y lo he hecho con mucho orgullo. ¡Que viva el Rey!

El hijo del rey oyó la conversación y, montando en su caballo, corrió tras ella. Pero el caballo de don Martín llegó primero al palacio del conde.

El conde estaba muy contento. Sabía que, gracias a su hija, él había cumplido con su deber.

El príncipe, al llegar a la puerta del castillo, llamó y preguntó por don Martín. Salió Catalina a recibirlo. Y él, dándose cuenta de quién era, se enamoró de ella instantáneamente. Y, dirigiéndose al conde, le pidió la mano de su hija en matrimonio.

Se dice que esta pareja vivió feliz por muchísimos años.

The Old Woman and the Candlestick

Don Pedro I (1334–1369), son and successor of Alfonso XI, was proclaimed king of Castile-Leon[1] in 1350. The young king was called The Cruel by his enemies and The Upholder of Justice by his friends. His reign was marked by constant civil war.

La vieja del candelero

Don Pedro I (1334–1369), hijo y sucesor de Alfonso XI, fue proclamado Rey de Castilla y León[1] en el año 1350. El joven rey fue llamado el Cruel por sus enemigos, pero fue conocido como el Justiciero por sus amigos. Su reinado estuvo marcado por constantes guerras civiles.

---

[1]Like Aragón, one of the kingdoms in which Spain was divided before its unification under King Ferdinand and Queen Isabella.

[1]Al igual que Aragón, Castilla y León era uno de los reinos en que se encontraba dividida España antes de su unificación por Fernando e Isabel.

*I*t was a dark night in Seville, a city in the south of Spain. No noise whatsoever was heard in the narrow street. All the neighbors slept, except for an old woman who lived alone in a humble little house.

Suddenly, she heard a clash of swords coming from the street corner. Shortly afterward, someone moaned in agony, "Help me, God. I'm dying!"

The old woman picked up a candlestick and went to the open window of her room. By the dim light of the candle she could see a man lying on the cobbled street. His body was covered with blood. By his side stood a tall, strong man with a sword in his hand. The light of the candle illuminated the face of the assassin.

At that moment, the old woman decided to withdraw from the window, but as luck would have it, her candlestick fell onto the street. The old woman hid behind the window curtains to listen. Soon she heard the footsteps of the assassin and the noise, which she recognized, of the arms that only certain people were permitted to use.

Hearing that strange noise, she knew the assassin was the gentleman who walked under her window every night at the same time. The old woman had seen him more than once and she knew who he was.

"Heavens!" she exclaimed.

Two or three hours later, a patrol passed by the scene of the murder. Immediately the guards informed the judge that a crime had been committed. They also gave him the candlestick near the cadaver.

The following day, King Pedro called for the judge and asked, "Last night a crime was committed in Seville, correct?"

"Yes, Your Majesty. The patrol found a man stabbed to death, with a candlestick by his side."

"Have you found the assassin?"

"Unfortunately, we have no leads. I have been working many hours on this case."

"You stupid fool!" the king said. "You haven't found any witnesses yet?"

ra una noche oscura en Sevilla, ciudad del sur de España. No se oía ningún ruido en la calle angosta. Todos los vecinos dormían ya, sin duda, menos una viejecita que vivía sola en una casita muy pobre.

De repente, se oyó un choque de espadas en la esquina de la calle. Poco después, una voz gritó en agonía:

—¡Válgame Dios! ¡Me muero!

La viejecita cogió el candelero y fue a una ventana abierta de su cuarto. Con la débil luz de la vela pudo ver a un hombre tendido sobre la calle empedrada. Su cuerpo estaba bañado en sangre. A su lado, estaba parado un hombre alto y fuerte que tenía una espada en la mano. La luz del candelero iluminó la cara del asesino.

En ese momento la viejecita decidió retirarse de la ventana; pero, por esas cosas del azar, el candelero se le cayó a la calle. La viejecita se escondió detrás de las cortinas de la ventana para escuchar. Pronto oyó las pisadas del asesino y el ruido, que ya conocía bien, de las armas que sólo a ciertas personas se les permitía usar.

Por ese ruido tan extraño, ella supo que el asesino era el caballero que pasaba todas las noches a la misma hora debajo de su ventana. La viejecita lo había visto más de una vez y sabía quién era.

—¡Santo Dios! —exclamó ella.

Dentro de dos o tres horas pasó por allí una ronda de vigilancia. Inmediatamente los guardias dieron al juez la noticia de que se había cometido un crimen. También le dieron el candelero que habían encontrado cerca del cadáver.

Al día siguiente, el rey Don Pedro llamó al juez y le preguntó:

—Anoche se cometió un crimen en Sevilla, ¿no?

—Sí, Su Majestad. La ronda encontró a un hombre muerto de una estocada y a su lado un candelero.

—¿Ha encontrado al asesino?

—Por desgracia, no tenemos ninguna pista todavía. He estado trabajando muchas horas en el asunto.

—¡Qué estúpido es usted! —exclamó el rey—. ¿Y no ha encontrado a ningún testigo?

"The neighbors living around the crime scene say they know absolutely nothing, that they heard nothing, that they cannot say anything. There is no witness except for the candlestick, and the candlestick cannot speak."

"But its owner can! If tonight you cannot find out who the owner of the candlestick is, tomorrow for certain you will lose your head."

One hour later the judge and the patrol visited all the people who lived near the crime scene, searching for the owner of the candlestick. Finally, they knocked on the old woman's door.

"Do you recognize this candlestick?" the judge asked her.

"Yes, it's mine," the old woman responded, frightened.

"Then you must accompany us to the palace to talk with the king."

They took her to a large room in King Don Pedro's palace. At that moment a person wrapped in a black cape came in. The old woman, who had her back to him, heard the footsteps and the noise of his weapon and exclaimed, "He's the one who killed the man near my house."

The old woman's words alarmed everyone in the room. They all said, "The king? That's impossible!"

"Yes, the king," Don Pedro repeated. "The old woman is telling the truth. Every night I walk around secretly through the streets of Seville to see if the patrol is obeying my orders. Last night when a drunk tried to kill me, I, in turn, killed him. That's how I committed the crime."

"Long live the king!" shouted the people in the large room.

"To show you that the king knows how to reward those who serve him well, I am going to give this woman a purse with one hundred gold coins."

The old woman thought she must be dreaming as she clutched the gift.

Then the king continued, "As you know, men cannot punish the king, only God can."

—Los vecinos próximos a la escena del crimen dicen que no saben absolutamente nada, ni han oído nada, ni nada pueden decir. No hay más testigo que un candelero y el candelero no habla.

—¡Pero, podrá hablar su dueño! Si esta noche no se sabe quién es el dueño del candelero, mañana usted perderá la cabeza.

Una hora después, el juez y la ronda visitaron a toda la gente que vivía cerca del lugar del crimen en busca del dueño del candelero. Al fin, llamaron a la puerta de la viejecita.

—¿Reconoce usted este candelero? —preguntó el juez.

—Sí, es mío —dijo la viejecita asustada.

—Entonces tendrá que ir al palacio con nosotros y hablar con el rey.

La llevaron a un salón grande del palacio del rey Don Pedro. En ese momento, entró una persona envuelta en una capa negra. La viejecita, que estaba de espaldas, oyó sus pisadas y el ruido de sus armas y exclamó:

—Ése que entró fue el que mató al hombre cerca de mi casa.

Las palabras de la viejecita alarmaron a los oyentes. Todos exclamaron:

—¿El rey? ¡No es posible!

—Sí, el rey —repitió Don Pedro—. La viejecita dice la verdad. Todas las noches me paseo secretamente por las calles de Sevilla para observar si la ronda está obedeciendo mis órdenes. Anoche, cuando un borracho trató de matarme, yo lo maté. Así fue como cometí el crimen.

—¡Viva el Rey! —gritó la gente en el salón.

—Como su rey sabe premiar a quien le sirve bien, voy a dar a esta mujer una bolsa con cien monedas de oro.

La viejecita creyó que estaba soñando mientras cogía el regalo.

Entonces continuó el rey:

—Como ustedes saben, los hombres no pueden castigar al rey, sólo Dios lo puede hacer.

The Bridge of St. Martin in Toledo

Toledo, situated on the banks of the Tajo River, was the capital of Spain many years ago. Now it is the capital of the province of Toledo. In times past, people of many cultures lived there, including Christians, Moors,[1] and Jews. Toledo is also known for a famous painter of Greek origin who adopted the city as his own: El Greco.[2] This artist was born in Crete in 1541, but spent his last years in Toledo, where he died in 1614. One of his most famous paintings is "Toledo," where he portrays his beloved city on a dark and rainy night.

El puente de San Martín en Toledo

Toledo, situado a orillas del Río Tajo, fue hace muchos años capital de España. Ahora es la capital de la provincia de Toledo. En tiempos pasados, vivieron allí pacíficamente gentes de diferentes culturas: cristianos, moros[1] y judíos. Pero Toledo es también conocido por un famoso pintor de origen griego que adoptó la ciudad como suya: El Greco.[2] Este artista, nacido en Creta en 1541, pasó sus últimos años en Toledo, donde murió en 1614. Uno de sus cuadros más conocidos es el *Toledo*, donde pinta a su querida ciudad en una noche oscura y lluviosa.

---

[1]The Moors were Muslims.
[2]The artist's name was Domenikos Theotokopoulos.

[1]Los moros eran mahometanos (o musulmanes).
[2]El pintor se llamaba Domenikos Theotokopoulos.

any, many years ago, the mayor of Toledo wanted to reconstruct the main bridge of the city. He sent messengers in search of the best architect of that time, and when he found him, he explained that he wanted the best bridge in Spain. The architect took his work very seriously, and the preparations took a long time. He also looked for the best workmen possible.

Finally, they began the work on the construction of the bridge. All the inhabitants of Toledo were satisfied and very happy about the sturdy, beautiful bridge being constructed. They anxiously awaited the completion of the project. At last, the architect and the workmen had finished the great arch and were preparing to remove the wooden frame that supported it.

But that night the architect could not sleep.

"What's the matter?" his wife asked.

"Oh, it's nothing, my dear. Go back to sleep," said the architect. But something was bothering him. That afternoon, after examining the wooden frame, he realized he had made a major mistake. He was sure that when the wooden frame was removed, the whole bridge would fall.

"I know something is wrong," the wife insisted. "What is it?"

"My dear, I don't know what to do. I have made a big mistake in the calculations for the bridge. I know that it is going to fall when the wooden frame is removed. What do you advise me to do?"

"You must talk to the mayor," the wife said, "and explain everything to him."

"But I can't. I have done something terrible. He won't understand. He will throw me in jail."

"It's the only thing you can do."

When the morning light came, the sky was cloudy. The architect left his house to talk with the mayor. The sky suddenly began to flash lightning and to thunder. At the mayor's house, he knocked at the door. The mayor came out and, at that moment, a terrible flash of lightning appeared in the sky, followed by the lights of a great fire. People were shouting, "The bridge is burning!"

*H*ace ya muchísimos años, el alcalde de Toledo quiso reconstruir el puente principal de la ciudad. Despachó mensajeros en busca del mejor arquitecto de aquel tiempo y cuando lo encontró, le explicó que quería construir el mejor puente de España. El arquitecto tomó muy en serio su trabajo y tardó mucho tiempo en preparar el plano y en buscar los mejores trabajadores.

Finalmente, se pusieron a trabajar en la construcción del puente. Todos los habitantes de Toledo estaban contentos y satisfechos del puente que se construía: un puente fuerte y hermoso. Esperaban ansiosamente la terminación del trabajo. Al fin, el arquitecto y los trabajadores habían terminado el gran arco y se preparaban para quitar la cimbra[3] que lo sostenía.

Pero esa noche, el arquitecto no pudo dormir.

—¿Qué te pasa? —le preguntó su esposa.

—No es nada, querida, duérmete —contestó el arquitecto. Pero sí había algo. Esa tarde, al examinar la cimbra, se dio cuenta de que había cometido un gran error. Al quitar la cimbra, él estaba seguro de que iba a caer todo el puente.

—Yo sé que algo te pasa —insistió su esposa—. ¿Qué es?

—Querida mía, no sé qué hacer. He cometido un grave error en los cálculos del puente. Sé que se va a caer al quitar la cimbra. ¿Qué me aconsejas?

—Debes hablar con el alcalde —dijo la esposa— y explicarle todo.

—Pero no puedo. He hecho algo terrible. Él no comprenderá. Me echará a la cárcel.

—Es lo único que puedes hacer.

Cuando apareció la luz del día, el cielo se estaba nublando. El arquitecto salió de la casa para ir a hablar con el alcalde. Comenzó a relampaguear y a tronar. Al llegar a la casa del alcalde, llamó a la puerta. Salió el alcalde y en ese momento se vio un relámpago terrible en el cielo, seguido por las luces de un gran incendio. Entonces oyeron a la gente gritar:

—¡El puente se enciende!

---

[3]Arco provisorio de madera que sostiene la estructura.

The bridge was indeed burning; the lightning had set it on fire.

The mayor and the architect ran toward the bridge. At the scene, the architect felt a mixture of sadness and gratitude. He felt sad that all his work was lost, and he felt grateful that he would not have to explain his error.

At noon, the bridge was in ruins. Not one stone remained standing. But the architect could not remain silent. He had to confess his error to the mayor.

"Mayor, I am to blame for everything."

But the mayor refused to believe him and would not let him continue. He kept saying, "The lightning did it. We shall have to build it all over again."

The architect accompanied the mayor to his house, intent on explaining his error with the bridge. Finally the mayor, somewhat upset, asked him, "What do you want to tell me? Why do you insist so much?"

The architect explained everything and waited for a response.

"Unbelievable, unbelievable," the mayor repeated, very surprised but deeply impressed with the architect's honesty. "What's done is done," he finally said. "Now you may begin construction on another bridge."

After expressing his gratitude to the mayor, the architect ran home and embraced his wife, saying, "The new bridge shall be a monument to the good will of the mayor and the mercy of heaven."

Y en realidad, el puente se quemaba; el relámpago lo había incendiado.

El alcalde y el arquitecto salieron corriendo hacia el puente. Al llegar y ver la situación, el arquitecto sintió a un mismo tiempo dos emociones: tristeza y gratitud. Sintió tristeza porque todo su trabajo estaba perdido y sintió gratitud porque no tendría que dar explicación de su error.

A mediodía, el puente quedó en ruinas. No quedó ni una sola piedra sobre otra. Pero el arquitecto no pudo callarse. Tenía que confesar su error al alcalde.

—Señor alcalde, yo tengo la culpa de todo.

Pero el alcalde no quería creerlo y no le dejaba continuar. Sólo seguía repitiendo:

—Fue el relámpago. Tendremos que reconstruir el puente otra vez.

El arquitecto acompañó al alcalde a su casa intentando explicarle su error con el puente. Al fin, el alcalde, algo molesto, le preguntó:

—¿Qué me quiere decir? ¿Por qué insiste tanto?

El arquitecto le explicó todo y esperó la contestación del alcalde.

—Increíble, increíble —repetía el alcalde sorprendido, pero a la vez impresionado por la honradez del arquitecto—. Lo que pasó, pasó —dijo al fin—. Ahora usted empezará de nuevo a construir otro.

Después de expresarle al alcalde su gratitud, el arquitecto corrió a su casa y, abrazando a su esposa, le dijo:

—El nuevo puente será monumento a la buena voluntad del alcalde y a la misericordia del cielo.

Casilda's Roses

Some Moorish kings were very cruel to the Christians in Spain,[1] locking them up in prisons, sometimes mistreating and even torturing them. Other Moorish kings, however, had a reputation for being tolerant and understanding, permitting the Christians to live on Moorish lands in complete peace. The legend that follows tells of Zenón, one of the cruelest kings Valencia had ever seen.

Las rosas de Casilda

En España hubo reyes moros[1] que fueron muy crueles con los cristianos de la península. A muchos los encerraban en sus prisiones: a veces los maltrataban y hasta los torturaban. En cambio, hubo otros reyes moros muy tolerantes y comprensivos que dejaban a los cristianos vivir en paz en tierras moras. La leyenda que sigue nos cuenta acerca de Zenón, uno de los reyes más crueles que ha visto Valencia.

---

[1]As already mentioned, the Moors were Muslims.

[1]Como anteriormente se mencionara, los moros eran de religión mahometana.

Zenón, the Moorish king of Valencia, had a daughter who possessed all the virtues her father lacked. He was stingy, cruel, and ferocious, while she was generous, kind, and compassionate.

The princess was named Casilda. She was one of the most beautiful women in Spain. Her father loved her dearly and tried to please her every whim.

Although the princess lived in the tallest tower of the castle, one night she happened to hear the echo of the shouts and laments of the Christians who were suffering in the castle prisons. She asked her father, "Father, where do all those cries and laments come from?"

But her father refused to answer.

She also asked the servants, but they gave her a horrified look and put a finger to their lips, as if to hush her.

"Do not ask anymore, princess," they said.

Casilda did not ask anymore, but day and night she had only one desire—to find the source of that suffering.

At nightfall, she got out of bed silently and went down the great stairway toward the source of the laments. Two Moorish soldiers stood before one of the prison doors. The princess took out two gold coins and gave each soldier one coin, saying, "Allah, and let me through! I am the princess Casilda."

The soldiers accepted the coins and opened the door. She entered. She was horrified to see so many people—men, women, and children—half-naked and hungry, some sick, others dying. Then Casilda understood that they were imprisoned because of their religion. She ran to her room and cried all night.

The next morning she confronted her father.

"Father, now I know where those cries and laments that I hear every night come from. If you love me, why not free the Christians?"

"Be quiet! Get out of here! Don't say another word or you shall die!"

Zenón, rey moro de Valencia, tenía una hija con todas las virtudes de que carecía su padre. Él era avaro, cruel y feroz, mientras que su hija era generosa, amable y compasiva.

La princesa se llamaba Casilda. Era una de las mujeres más bellas de España. Su padre la amaba tiernamente y trataba de complacerla en todos sus caprichos.

Pues sucedió que la princesa, aunque tenía sus habitaciones en la torre más alta del castillo, llegó a oír por las noches el eco de los gritos y lamentos de los cristianos que sufrían en las prisiones del castillo. Entonces, ella le preguntó a su padre:

—Papá, ¿de dónde vienen tantos gritos y lamentos?

Pero su padre no quiso responder.

Ella también preguntó a sus criadas, pero ellas, con una expresión de horror, se llevaron un dedo a los labios.

—No preguntes más, princesita —dijeron ellas.

Casilda no preguntó más, pero día y noche tenía sólo un deseo: el deseo de descubrir el secreto de esos gritos de sufrimiento.

Cuando fue de noche, se levantó de la cama silenciosamente y bajó la gran escalera hacia donde venían los lamentos. Dos soldados moros estaban delante de una puerta de la prisión. La princesa sacó dos monedas de oro y dio una a cada uno y dijo:

—Alá y paso franco,[2] que soy la princesa Casilda.

Los soldados aceptaron las monedas y abrieron la puerta. Ella entró. Pero quedó horrorizada al ver a tanta gente —hombres, mujeres y niños— medio desnudos y hambrientos, unos enfermos, otros moribundos. Entonces Casilda comprendió que por su religión estaban en las prisiones. Salió corriendo a su cuarto y lloró toda la noche.

A la mañana siguiente fue a hablar con su padre.

—Padre mío, ahora sé de dónde salen esos gritos y lamentos que oigo todas las noches. Si usted me quiere, ¿por qué no suelta a los cristianos?

—¡Cállate! ¡Sal de aquí! ¡No digas más o morirás!

---

[2]Fórmula utilizada para pedir u ordenar libre pasaje.

The princess could not believe her father's words. She wept inconsolably, ran to her room, and decided to help the Christians.

From that day on, she carried food for the prisoners inside her apron and coins for the Moorish soldiers.

One morning, when Casilda was going to the prison with her apron full of food, she met the king, her father.

"Good morning, daughter. Where are you off to so early and in such a hurry?" the king said, trying to hide the disdain he felt for Casilda.

"Father," the daughter answered, "you have always told me that the gardens are most beautiful in the morning, and today I went to see them."

"And the morning air has put the most beautiful roses in your cheeks," the king said.

The princess was going to continue her walk when the king noticed the large bundle that Casilda was carrying in her apron.

"What do you have in your apron? Is it something for the prisoners? Answer!"

Without a moment's hesitation, and anticipating her father's anger, the princess turned and opened her apron. A bunch of white and yellow roses fell to the ground. The king, seeing the surprised look on his daughter's face, realized that he had witnessed a miracle. He embraced his daughter and said, weeping, "This very day I am freeing all the prisoners, and I am going to sign a peace treaty with the Christians."

La princesa no pudo creer las palabras de su padre. Llorando desconsoladamente, llegó a su cuarto y decidió ayudar a los cristianos.

Desde aquel día llevaba dentro de su delantal abundante comida para los prisioneros y monedas para los soldados moros.

Una mañana, cuando iba Casilda a la prisión con su delantal lleno de comida, encontró al rey, su padre.

—Buenos días, hija. ¿Adónde vas tan temprano y con tanta prisa? —dijo el rey, tratando de esconder el desdén que sintió por Casilda.

—Papá —contestó la hija—, usted siempre me ha dicho que los jardines son más bellos por la mañana y hoy fui a verlos.

—Y el aire de la mañana ha puesto las más bellas rosas en tu cara —dijo el rey.

Iba la princesa a continuar su camino cuando el rey notó el gran bulto que llevaba Casilda en su delantal.

—¿Qué llevas ahí dentro de tu delantal? ¿Es algo para los prisioneros? ¡Responde!

Y la princesa, sin vacilar un momento, esperando la ira de su padre, volteó y abrió el delantal. Un ramillete de rosas blancas y amarillas cayó al suelo. El rey, viendo la cara de sorpresa de su hija, se dio cuenta del milagro. Abrazó a su hija y le dijo llorando:

—Hoy mismo daré libertad a todos los prisioneros y voy a firmar un tratado de paz con los cristianos.

The Mysterious Drawer

Madrid is today a modern, cosmopolitan city with a rich history and culture. Its streets have many fascinating stories to tell. One such street is Santa Isabel Street, where once lived a lady of extraordinary beauty named Prudencia Grilo. On that same street there was also a convent. Doña Prudencia, who had been a flirtatious young lady with many suitors, ultimately became the Mother Superior of this convent. This legend narrates what happened to her and to the suitor with whom she fell in love and wanted to marry.

El cajón misterioso

El Madrid de hoy es una ciudad moderna y cosmopolita con una rica historia y tradición. Sus calles tienen tantas cosas fascinantes que contar. Una de estas calles es la calle de Santa Isabel, donde una vez vivió una dama de extraordinaria belleza llamada Prudencia Grilo. En esta misma calle había también un convento. Doña Prudencia, que había sido muy coqueta y había tenido muchísimos pretendientes, llegó a ser Madre Superiora de este convento. Esta leyenda narra lo que ocurrió con ella y el pretendiente de quien se enamoró y con quien quiso casarse.

*A*lthough Prudencia flirted with all of her suitors, she finally fell in love with a handsome lieutenant from Andalusia, and they decided to get married. She did not realize what it meant to be the wife of a soldier and lived in the idyllic, romantic world of love. Although all of these events took place in the sixteenth century, they could well have taken place in our time.

Doña Prudencia was very surprised when her husband-to-be came to tell her that they would have to postpone the wedding because he had to go to war to fight against England. As a soldier, he could not refuse the opportunity to serve Spain and, besides, he could earn glory and fame to bestow upon his king and his future wife.

Although extremely sad and thinking that all this must be just a bad dream, Prudencia knew that she could do nothing but wait. Still in an emotional state, the two kissed, thinking about their future wedding that would take place after the war.

"How will I get news from you? How will I know how you are doing and when you will return?" Prudencia asked.

"A letter would never get to you now that we are at war, but I will tell you how you will get news of me. If you don't receive any message, know that I am well. Otherwise, the desk that is next to your bedroom will give you a sign."

"But how? I don't understand," she said.

"If I should be killed, one of the drawers will open all by itself."

"But that is a very strange sign! I don't want to even think about it."

"Nevertheless, that's how it will be," he responded.

They hugged and kissed thinking about how happy they would be after the war, together as a married couple. Sadly, they said good-bye. He was thinking of the honors he would win for Spain, and she thought about how sad farewells were. The fiancé, Don Martín Ávila, acted bravely because he didn't want her to know that he was also grieving about having to go off to war. He knew that there was a possibility that he would never return.

Aunque doña Prudencia coqueteaba con todos sus pretendientes, al fin se enamoró de un teniente andaluz bastante guapo y los dos decidieron casarse. Ella no se daba cuenta de lo que significaba ser esposa de un soldado y vivía en un mundo romántico e idílico. Todo esto ocurrió en el siglo XVI, pero bien podría haber sucedido en nuestros tiempos.

Doña Prudencia quedó muy sorprendida cuando su novio vino a anunciarle que tendrían que posponer la boda porque él tenía que ir a la guerra contra Inglaterra. Como era soldado, no podía rechazar la oportunidad de servir a España. Así también podía ganar gloria y fama para brindarles a su rey y a su futura esposa.

Sumamente triste y creyendo que todo no era más que una horrible pesadilla, ella sabía que nada podía hacer sino esperar. Todavía en ese estado emocional, los dos se besaron, pensando en la boda que vendría después de la guerra.

—¿Cómo sabré de ti, cómo te va y cuándo regresarás? —preguntó Prudencia.

—Una carta no te llegará nunca, ya que estaremos en guerra. Pero te diré cómo sabrás de mí. Si no recibes ningún mensaje, sabrás que estoy bien. Si no, ese escritorio que está al lado de tu dormitorio te dará la señal.

—¿Pero cómo? No entiendo... —dijo ella.

—En caso de que me toque morir, uno de los cajones se abrirá por sí mismo.

—¡Qué señal más extraña! No quiero ni pensar en eso.

—Pero así será —contestó.

Se abrazaron y se besaron y otra vez pensaron en lo feliz que serían cuando terminara la guerra, ya juntos y casados. Tristemente, se despidieron: él pensando en ganar gloria para España y ella en cuán tristes eran las despedidas. Martín Ávila, el novio, fingió valentía porque no quería que ella se diera cuenta de que él también lamentaba el hecho de tener que ir a la guerra. Él sabía que existía la posibilidad de que no volviera.

Several days later, the flotilla of ships known as the "Invincible Armada" left port en route to England.

Counting the days, Prudencia never stopped thinking about Martín and the perils of war. Weeks passed and no message came. She began to feel happy, knowing that this meant all was well. But one day, while in bed, she heard a noise from the room next door. She got up and went to see what it was. Horrified, she saw that it was the desk. One of the drawers was opening by itself. Prudencia, very upset and feeling as if she were about to die, knew what it meant—Martín had been killed!

Inconsolable, she could only think of Martín, his noble intentions, and the great sacrifice he had made. She also thought about how happy the two of them would have been together for the rest of their lives. She would never recover from Martín's death.

Now that she was alone, there was nothing else that Prudencia could do but think about her own future. Finally, she decided to become a nun and entered the convent on Santa Isabel Street where, in time, she became the Mother Superior.

It is said that in the chapel of the convent, Prudencia, as Mother Superior, ordered that an empty coffin be placed in memory of Martín and what could have been for the two of them.

Días después salió del puerto rumbo a Inglaterra la flota conocida como La Armada Invencible.

Prudencia, sin olvidar nunca a su querido Martín, contaba los días, siempre pensando en él y en el peligro de la guerra. Pasaron semanas y no recibió ningún mensaje. Comenzó a sentirse feliz, porque sabía que eso indicaba que todo andaba bien. Pero un día, estando en la cama, oyó un ruido que venía del cuarto de al lado. Se levantó y fue a ver lo que causaba ese ruido. Horrorizada, vio que era el escritorio. Uno de los cajones se abría solo. Prudencia, entonces, muy turbada y sintiendo que se moría, sabía lo que el cajón le indicaba: Martín estaba muerto.

Desconsolada, no podía sino pensar en Martín y lo noble que fueron sus intenciones y el gran sacrificio que hizo. También pensaba en lo feliz que podían haber sido, casados y juntos por el resto de sus vidas. Nunca iba a recuperarse de la muerte de Martín.

Ahora que quedaba sola, no había nada que Prudencia pudiera hacer sino pensar en su propio futuro. Finalmente, decidió hacerse monja y entró en el convento de la calle de Santa Isabel, donde con el tiempo llegó a ser Madre Superiora.

Se dice que en la capilla del convento, Prudencia, la nueva Madre Superiora, mandó colocar un ataúd vacío en memoria de la muerte de Martín y de lo que pudo haber sido para los dos.

The Student of Salamanca

The University of Salamanca,[1] founded around 1220 by King Alfonso IX, enjoyed a period of great splendor in the sixteenth century. During these years, more than ten thousand students from Spain and around the world attended classes there. This prestigious university offered a variety of courses, such as medicine, law, music, astronomy, philosophy, and religion. Even Christopher Columbus went there once to talk to the professors about his trip to discover a direct route to India. In the university, there were also many poor students such as the one described in this legend.

El estudiante de Salamanca

La Universidad de Salamanca,[1] fundada hacia 1220 por el Rey Alfonso IX, conoció en el siglo XVI un período de gran esplendor. Durante estos años, más de diez mil alumnos venidos de España y de países extranjeros estudiaron en esta universidad. Esta prestigiosa institución ofrecía una gran variedad de cursos: medicina, leyes, música, astronomía, filosofía y religión. Incluso Cristóbal Colón fue en una ocasión a la universidad para hablar con los profesores acerca del viaje que quería hacer para descubrir una ruta directa a la India. En la universidad, había muchos estudiantes pobres como el joven de esta leyenda.

---

[1]The University of Salamanca was one of the first universities in Europe. It is located in Salamanca, a town northwest of Madrid.

[1]La Universidad de Salamanca fue una de las primeras universidades de Europa. Está situada en Salamanca, una ciudad al noroeste de Madrid.

*I*n many Spanish-speaking countries, children don't receive gifts on Christmas day but on the sixth of January: the Feast of the Three Wise Men.[2] On the night before, before going to bed, they place their shoes outside the doorway, on the balcony, or at an open window. In the silence of the night, the Three Wise Men come and fill their shoes with toys and candy. They say that these are the same Wise Men who brought gifts to the child Jesus in Bethlehem.

One day in December when it was raining very heavily, a poor student, dressed in rags, entered a shoe shop and said to the shoemaker, "Good morning, sir. Look at these shoes. These are my little brother's only shoes. How worn they are! Can you make him a new pair?"

"Yes, of course, that's my job. How old is the boy?"

"He's five years old and he thinks he's going to get new shoes from the Three Wise Men. For that reason, I need them before the sixth of January."

"Very well. Come back in four days and the shoes will be ready."

After four days, the student came back. Upon receiving the well-made shoes, he exclaimed, "Oh, what beautiful work! How much do I owe you?"

"Nothing, absolutely nothing," replied the shoemaker. "It's a gift for your little brother."

"A thousand thanks, sir. You are always very kind to my family. We are poor but, someday, when I am Archbishop of Toledo,[3] I shall be able to give you a generous gift."

"Very well," answered the shoemaker with a smile. "I think I'll have to wait quite a while. But come back and see me if I can be of any service to you."

Years went by and the shoemaker, now much older, could no longer work, and he lived in poverty.

---

[2]Also known as the Three Kings.
[3]The highest ecclesiastic position in the Catholic Church in Spain.

En muchos de los países de habla hispana, los niños no reciben regalos en la Navidad sino el seis de enero: Día de Reyes. La noche previa, antes de acostarse, ellos ponen sus zapatitos en la puerta, en el balcón o en una ventana abierta. En el silencio de la noche vienen los tres Reyes Magos y llenan los zapatitos de juguetes y dulces. Se dice que son los mismos reyes que trajeron regalos al Niño Jesús en Belén.

Un día de diciembre en que llovía a cántaros, un pobre estudiante vestido en harapos, entró en la tienda de un zapatero en Salamanca y le dijo:

—Muy buenos días, señor. Mire usted estos zapatos. Son los únicos que tiene mi hermanito. ¡Qué mal están! ¿Puede usted hacerle otros nuevos?

—Sí, señor, es mi trabajo. ¿Cuántos años tiene el chico?

—Tiene cinco años y cree que va a recibir zapatos nuevos de los Reyes Magos. Por eso, los necesito para antes del seis de enero.

—Muy bien. Vuelva usted en cuatro días y los zapatitos estarán listos.

Pasados los cuatro días, el estudiante regresó. Al recibir los zapatos tan bonitos, exclamó:

—¡Ay, qué trabajo tan excelente! ¿Cuánto le debo a usted?

—Nada, absolutamente nada —respondió el zapatero—. Es un regalito para su hermano.

—Mil gracias, señor. Usted es siempre tan amable con mi familia. Somos pobres; pero, cuando yo sea Arzobispo de Toledo,[2] voy a poder darle un generoso regalo.

—Está bien —replicó el zapatero, con una sonrisa—. Creo que tendré que esperar un largo tiempo. Pero, vuelva usted a visitarme si puedo servirle en algo.

Pasaron los años y el zapatero, ya muy anciano, no podía trabajar y vivía en la pobreza.

---

[2]La más alta distinción dentro de la jerarquía católica de España.

One day, a priest came to the shoe shop and asked the old man to accompany him to the palace of the Archbishop of Toledo. The shoemaker was very frightened and didn't want to go. Overcoming his fear, he set out with the priest. In the presence of the Archbishop, the Archbishop spoke to him very affectionately, "My friend, many years ago you made a pair of shoes for my little brother when I was a student at the University of Salamanca. I was very poor then, but your generosity impressed me greatly. You will remember I promised you on that occasion a generous gift when I became Archbishop of Toledo. Well, now I am, and I want to give you the price of the shoes. A good deed never goes unrewarded."

And he gave the old man a bag containing fifty ounces of gold coins.

"Also, my fine shoemaker," he continued, "whatever you want, anything, just ask me in full confidence and I shall try to grant your wish."

Crying from happiness, the shoemaker replied, "Sir, I can hardly believe what is happening to me. The money which you have just given me will last me the rest of my life. The only thing I could possibly ask for is that when I die, my two daughters not be abandoned."

"That shall be taken care of in short order," assured the Archbishop.

"God bless you!" answered the shoemaker.

After some time, the Archbishop founded the College for Noble Young Women. Its first students were the shoemaker's daughters, to whom the Archbishop had given titles of nobility.

Un día, se presentó en la zapatería un cura que le pidió al viejecito que lo acompañara al palacio del Arzobispo de Toledo. El zapatero tenía mucho miedo y no quería ir. Pero, venciendo su temor, se puso en camino con el cura. Al presentarse ante el Arzobispo, éste, en tono muy cariñoso, le dijo:

—Amigo mío, hace muchos años usted me dio un par de zapatos para mi hermano cuando yo era estudiante en Salamanca. Yo era muy pobre en aquel entonces y me conmovió su generosidad. Usted se acordará de que en esa misma ocasión le había prometido un generoso regalo cuando fuera Arzobispo de Toledo. Ahora lo soy y aquí tiene usted el precio de los zapatos. Las buenas acciones son siempre recompensadas.

Y le dio al viejecito una bolsa en que había cincuenta onzas de oro.

—También, señor zapatero —continuó el Arzobispo—, si quiere pedirme cualquier cosa, hágalo con toda confianza y trataré de otorgársela.

Llorando de felicidad, el zapatero contestó:

—Señor, apenas puedo creer lo que me pasa. El dinero que usted acaba de regalarme me basta para vivir bien el resto de mi vida. Sólo deseo que a mi muerte no queden abandonadas dos hijas que tengo.

—Usted verá cumplidos sus deseos muy pronto —prometió el Arzobispo.

—¡Que Dios lo bendiga! —respondió el zapatero.

Poco tiempo después, el Arzobispo de Toledo fundó el Colegio de Doncellas Nobles, cuyas primeras alumnas fueron las hijas del zapatero, a las que el Arzobispo había dado títulos de nobleza.

12

Pedro de Urdemalas

When the Spaniards came to the New World, they brought with them not only their religion, music, art, industry, and customs, but also their stories and legends. Among the best known characters in this type of tale is Pedro de Urdemalas,[1] a rogue without equal. During the sixteenth and seventeenth centuries, the picaresque novel was very popular in Spain.

Pedro de Urdemalas

Cuando los españoles llegaron al Nuevo Mundo, trajeron consigo no sólo su religión, su música, su arte, industrias y costumbres, sino también sus cuentos y leyendas. Entre los personajes más conocidos de este tipo de narración está Pedro de Urdemalas, un pícaro sin igual.[1] Durante los siglos XVI y XVII, la novela picaresca fue muy popular en España.

---

[1] Another well-known picaresque character is Lazarillo de Tormes.

[1] Otro personaje muy conocido es el Larazillo de Tormes.

*P*edro de Urdemalas was born in Segovia,[2] Spain. For that reason, according to his mother, he was pure Castilian, even though he carried in his veins the blood of the Iberians, the Visigoths, and the Phoenicians, mixed with some Roman and Arabic blood. And this mixture of blood was only on his mother's side, since his father was German.

Pedro's mother was Juana González. She was a pretty woman. Her husband had abandoned her shortly before Pedro was born. When naming the child, the mother remembered that *ur* in German means "cause" or "source." Therefore, she indicated that the child's last name should be Ur de males, that is, "source of troubles." His first name was Pedro because he was born on Saint Pedro's day. So everyone started to call him mockingly Don Pedro de Urdemalas.

According to the legend, Pedro was born with a gold tooth. No one knows whether this is true. But we do know that he was an extraordinary child.

When Pedro was only five years old, he went with his stepfather, a shepherd, to help tend the sheep. After seven years, he sought work with a rich neighbor named Remigio Ortiz. He served this master for six years, helping him tend his pigs.

At the end of this time, Pedro decided he should be earning more than the few coins per month that he received from the rich Señor Ortiz.

So one morning he went to a merchant and asked him if he wanted to buy fifty fat pigs from his master.

"Yes, I'd like that. When can you deliver them to me?"

"Tomorrow I'll come with the pigs, sir," Pedro responded. "But I'll have to sell them to you without their tails. My master has offered the tails to Saint Carolampio[3] to be used to cure a fever."

"That's fine," the merchant answered, believing Pedro's lie about his master.

---

[2]City in Castile northwest of Madrid, famous for its Roman aqueduct.
[3]Fictitious saint humorously made up by Pedro.

*P*edro de Urdemalas nació en Segovia,[2] España. Por eso, según su madre, Pedro era castellano castizo, aunque llevaba en sus venas sangre de íberos, visigodos y fenicios mezclada con un poco de sangre romana y árabe. Esta mezcla de sangre le venía sólo por el lado de su madre, pues su padre era alemán.

La madre de Pedro se llamaba Juana González. Era una mujer bonita. Su esposo la había abandonado poco antes del nacimiento de Pedro. Al ponerle nombre al niño y recordando que *ur* en alemán significa "causa", la madre indicó que el apellido de su hijo era Ur de males, es decir, la causa de sus males. El nombre de pila del niño era Pedro porque había nacido el día de San Pedro. Así fue cómo la gente empezó a llamarle burlonamente don Pedro de Urdemalas.

Según la leyenda, Pedro nació con un diente de oro. Nadie sabe si es verdad o no. Pero sí se sabe que fue un niño extraordinario.

Cuando Pedro tenía sólo cinco años, fue con su padrastro, un pastor, para ayudarle con las ovejas. Después de siete años, buscó otro trabajo con un buen vecino rico llamado Remigio Ortiz. Durante seis años sirvió a su amo, ayudándole con el cuidado de los cerdos.

Pasados los seis años, Pedro creyó que debía tener más dinero que unos pocos duros al mes que recibía del rico señor Ortiz.

Así, una mañana fue a un comerciante y le preguntó si quería comprar cincuenta cerdos gordos a su patrón.

—Sí, con mucho gusto. ¿Cuándo puede entregármelos?

—Mañana vendré con los cerdos, señor —respondió Pedro—. Pero es necesario venderlos sin cola. Mi amo ha ofrecido las colas a San Carolampio[3] para curarse de una calentura.

—Está bien —respondió el comerciante que creyó la mentira que Pedro le había contado acerca de su patrón.

---

[2]Ciudad de Castilla, situada al noroeste de Madrid y conocida por su acueducto romano.
[3]Un santo ficticio que fue invento cómico de Pedro.

The next morning, Pedro cut the tails off all the pigs, keeping them in a sack. Later he turned the pigs over to the merchant and collected his money. Then he returned to his master's farm. He immediately hid the money in the woods and buried the tails in the mud at the edge of a small lake. Near the shore of the lake he also buried a pig that had died several days before, so that only its tail was visible.

Then Pedro went to his master to tell him that the pigs had fallen into the lake and that only their tails were visible. The master ran to the place. He tried to pull on the tail nearest him. Pedro helped him, and finally they pulled out the dead pig.

"Oh, what a shame! The poor pigs!" cried the master. "But what is lost, is lost."

Seeing that Pedro was very sad, the master didn't punish him. He said, "You can go home, young man. From now on I don't need your help."

"Very well, master; thank you for your kindness," Pedro said, crying.

When the master went home, Pedro went to the woods to recover his hidden money. There he stopped crying, of course.

The following week Pedro left his family and set out for the New World, where he continued his roguish adventures. It is said that, after two or three years, Pedro de Urdemalas changed his ways and became a man of good and noble qualities.

La mañana siguiente, Pedro cortó las colas de todos los cerdos y las guardó en una bolsa. Luego entregó los cerdos al comerciante y recibió el dinero. Entonces volvió a la hacienda de su amo. En seguida escondió el dinero en el bosque y colocó las colas en el lodo a la orilla de un pequeño lago. Cerca de la orilla colocó también un cerdo que había muerto hacía algunos días, de manera que sólo se veía la cola.

Luego Pedro fue a su amo a contarle que los cerdos habían caído al lago y que sólo se podían ver las colas. El amo corrió al lugar. Trató de sacar la cola que encontró más cerca. Pedro le ayudó y al fin sacaron al animal muerto.

—¡Ay, qué lástima! ¡Los pobres cerdos! —dijo el patrón—. Pero lo que se perdió, se perdió.

Al ver que Pedro estaba muy triste, el patrón, en vez de castigarle, le dijo:

—Puedes marcharte a tu casa, joven. De hoy en adelante ya no necesitaré de tus servicios.

—Bueno, don Remigio, y gracias por su bondad —contestó Pedro llorando.

Cuando el patrón se fue a su casa, Pedro se dirigió al bosque para recoger el dinero que había escondido. Allí paró de llorar, por supuesto.

La semana siguiente, Pedro dejó a su familia y salió para el Nuevo Mundo donde continuó sus pícaras aventuras. Se dice que, después de unos tres años, Pedro de Urdemalas cambió de vida y llegó a ser un hombre bondadoso y noble.

13

Murillo, the Famous Painter

Bartolomé Esteban Murillo (1618–1682) was born in Seville, where he spent his whole life, except for the three years he studied in Madrid with the great painter Velázquez.[1] Of all the Spanish painters, Murillo was the greatest idealist, and as a religious painter, he was unrivaled. In 1852, a painting called "The Immaculate Conception" was sold to the Louvre Museum in Paris for $120,000. The Prado Museum in Madrid, founded in 1819 by King Fernando VII, houses many famous paintings by the great artist Murillo.

Murillo, pintor famoso

Bartolomé Esteban Murillo (1618–1682) nació en Sevilla, donde vivió toda su vida excepto los tres años que estudió en Madrid con el gran pintor Diego de Velázquez.[1] De todos los pintores españoles, Murillo fue el más genial idealista; y, como pintor religioso, se dice que no tiene rival. En 1852 una pintura titulada *La Inmaculada Concepción* fue vendida al Museo del Louvre en París por 120,000 dólares. El Museo del Prado en Madrid, fundado en 1819 por el rey Fernando VII, posee muchos cuadros famosos pintados por el gran artista Murillo.

---

[1]Diego de Velázquez (1599–1660): one of the greatest Spanish painters, famous for his masterpiece "Las Meninas."

[1]Diego de Velásquez (1599–1660), uno de los grandes maestros de la pintura universal. Es autor de "Las Meninas".

*D*uring the first part of his life, Murillo, an orphan from childhood, was extremely poor. When he was ten years old, he went to a church in Seville to observe a famous artist who was painting religious scenes. The boy approached the painter and said, "Sir, someday I hope to paint religious scenes."

Looking at the sincere, intelligent boy, the artist answered him, "I believe you will because you have the image of God in your mind and in your heart."

Murillo never forgot the artist's words, and six years later he was earning his living by painting hundreds of small images of the Madonna.[2] He sold some of them in the markets and in the streets of Seville. Others were bought by churches in Mexico and Peru.

A legend tells us that Murillo worked for three years painting twenty pictures for a new convent in Seville. Everyone loved him there because he was humble and kind.

The monks chatted with him, the gardener brought him flowers, and the cook prepared special dishes for him. Everyone wanted to do something special for the great artist.

One day the cook came to his room and said, "Señor Murillo, I hear you are leaving us soon. Do you have a souvenir for your old friend, the cook? Can't you leave me a small picture?"

"Of course, my friend," the painter answered kindly. "Just give me a canvas; I don't have any left."

The cook didn't have a canvas either, but he was using a heavy napkin as an apron.

Murillo took the napkin and prepared it for painting. A few days later he called his faithful friend, the cook, and said to him as he gave him the napkin, "Take this picture. This kind of work cannot be bought with money, but with true friendship."

---

[2]The Virgin Mary.

*D*urante la primera etapa de su vida, Murillo, huérfano desde niño, fue muy pobre. Cuando tenía diez años, fue a una iglesia en Sevilla para observar a un artista famoso que estaba pintando escenas religiosas. El chico se acercó al pintor y le dijo:

—Señor, algún día yo también quiero pintar cuadros religiosos.

Viendo al niño tan sincero e inteligente, el artista le contestó:

—Tú lo puedes hacer, pequeño, porque creo que tienes la imagen de Dios en el pensamiento y en el corazón.

Murillo nunca olvidó las palabras del artista y seis años más tarde se ganaba la vida pintando centenares de pequeños cuadros de la Madona.[2] Vendió algunos en los mercados y en las calles de Sevilla. Otros cuadros fueron comprados por iglesias en México y en el Perú.

Una leyenda nos cuenta que Murillo trabajó durante tres años pintando veinte cuadros para un nuevo convento en Sevilla. Allí todos lo querían mucho porque este pintor era muy amable y sencillo.

Los monjes charlaban con él; el jardinero le regalaba flores; el cocinero le preparaba platos exquisitos. Todos querían hacer algo por el gran artista.

Un día llegó el cocinero a su cuarto y le dijo:

—Señor Murillo, he oído que muy pronto usted se marchará. ¿Tiene usted algún recuerdo para su amigo el viejo cocinero? ¿No puede usted dejarme algún dibujito suyo?

—Con mucho gusto, amigo —contestó el pintor amablemente—, pero déme usted un lienzo, porque ya no me quedan.

El cocinero tampoco tenía lienzo, pero llevaba de delantal una gruesa servilleta.

Murillo cogió la servilleta y la preparó bien. Algunos días después, llamó a su fiel amigo el cocinero y le dijo, dándole la servilleta:

—Tome usted su dibujito. Este trabajo no puede comprarse con dinero, pero sí con amistad verdadera.

---

[2]La Virgen María.

The cook looked at the napkin with tears of gratitude in his eyes. The great master had painted a beautiful Madonna with a child in her arms.

This painting is known today as "The Madonna of the Napkin." No artist has ever been able to surpass the magnificent colors of this masterpiece.

El cocinero miró la servilleta con lágrimas de gratitud. El gran maestro había pintado una hermosa Madona con un hermoso niño en los brazos.

Este cuadro se conoce hoy en día como *La Madona de la Servilleta*. Se dice que ningún artista ha podido sobrepasar los magníficos colores de esta obra maestra.

14

The Mercy Dagger

Madrid, located on Spain's central high plain, was a small town called Magerit during the time of the Moorish invasion. In the eleventh century, the Spaniards reconquered the area, and in the sixteenth century, Madrid was made the capital of the country. It was later occupied by the French for a short time during the first part of the nineteenth century. Madrid is the largest city in Spain and is the heart of the country.

El puñal de misericordia

Madrid, situado en la alta meseta central española, era un pequeño pueblo llamado Magerit en los tiempos de la invasión mora. En el siglo XI los españoles reconquistaron la región y en el siglo XVI Madrid fue hecha capital del país. Por corto tiempo, fue ocupada por los franceses a principios del siglo XIX. Madrid es la ciudad más grande de España y es el corazón del país.

*D*on Luis de Guzmán and his wife, Doña María, had one daughter, Marianita. Her beauty was known throughout the city of Madrid.

But something rather strange happened in the house of the Marquis Don Luis. It was never open to social events, and its owners never attended any social affairs. They always had an appropriate excuse. They didn't even go to official receptions held at the king's palace. It was a strange situation, considering that their daughter was beautiful and of marrying age. The only time they left the house was to hear mass in the nearby church.

Naturally, this situation was the cause of a great deal of gossip in the town. The family's solitary life was well known and the stories that traveled from lips to ears were many and varied.

Among the very few people who had been able to appreciate the exceptional beauty of Marianita during her church visits was Don Felipe de Rojas, a young noble whose family was friends of the king. Don Felipe had seen Marianita and had fallen in love with her. The only acknowledgment he had received from her was a slight inclination of the head when he greeted her. Nothing more.

Don Felipe was a quiet, serious person with good manners and good habits. Everyone respected him.

One day, after much thought, he sent his servant to the house of Don Luis, Marianita's father, requesting permission for a visit. The marquis agreed to the visit and asked that he come at five o'clock in the evening.

The young man arrived for the meeting punctually and greeted the marquis courteously.

"Sir," he said, "first my regards to your wife, the marquise, and to you; then I will state the purpose of my visit."

"Thank you," the marquis said. "Please be seated. I am anxious to know what you are going to say."

"For a long time now," the young man began, "I have been in love with your daughter, Marianita. I have come to formally ask for her hand."

The marquis turned pale for a few moments and then said, "Have you spoken with my daughter?"

Don Luis de Guzmán y su esposa, doña María, tenían una hija, Marianita. La fama de su belleza era conocida en todo Madrid.

Pero algo raro sucedía en la casa del marqués don Luis. Nunca se abría para fiestas. Tampoco asistían sus dueños a ninguna reunión social; siempre tenían una disculpa apropiada. Ni siquiera iban a las recepciones oficiales en el palacio del rey. Era una actitud extraña, considerando que Marianita era linda y estaba en edad de casarse. Las únicas veces que salían eran para oír misa en la iglesia cercana.

Naturalmente, tal situación fue causa de chisme entre la gente. El caso de su solitaria vida era bien conocido y los cuentos que corrían de labios a oídos eran muchos y muy variados.

Entre las pocas personas que habían podido apreciar la excepcional belleza de Marianita en sus idas a la iglesia estaba don Felipe de Rojas, un joven noble cuya familia era amiga del rey. Don Felipe había visto a Marianita y se había enamorado de ella. La única atención que él recibía de ella era sólo una ligera inclinación de la cabeza cuando él la saludaba. Nada más.

Don Felipe era un joven callado y serio, bien educado y de buenas costumbres. Todos lo respetaban.

Un día, después de pensarlo mucho, don Felipe envió a su criado a casa de don Luis, padre de Marianita, pidiéndole permiso para hacer una visita. El marqués accedió a su pedido, fijando la cita para las cinco de la tarde.

El joven llegó puntualmente a la cita y saludó cortésmente al marqués:

—Señor —dijo—, antes que nada mis respetos a su esposa, la marquesa, y a usted y luego el asunto de mi visita.

—Gracias —dijo el marqués—. Siéntese. Me interesa lo que me va a decir.

—Desde hace mucho tiempo —comenzó el joven— he estado enamorado de su hija, Marianita. Vengo a pedirle su mano oficialmente.

El marqués se puso pálido por unos momentos y luego respondió:

—¿Ha hablado usted con mi hija?

"No, Marquis," Felipe answered. "I have never had the opportunity. But I believe that my eyes have revealed my love to her and I believe that Marianita has understood it."

The marquis then told him, "You honor my house, but there is a great impediment. Since Marianita was a little girl, she has made a solemn vow not to marry."

Felipe could not speak. His gaze was fixed on the wall, where a beautiful mercy dagger hung. (Knights used these daggers to slay their conquered enemies or to sacrifice themselves rather than be humiliated in defeat.)

The young man knew that under such a vow, Marianita would not change her mind. Without saying a word, the young man got up and went toward the door. Slowly and sadly the young man said to the marquis, "You have taken my life from me. That dagger on the wall could not have done it better."

"I am very sorry, Don Felipe. But I too am suffering," said the marquis.

Don Felipe left the house and crossed the street. He looked toward the house as if to say good-bye, and as he did, he thought he saw a face in one of the windows. A flutter of hope entered his soul. He could not move from that spot, and an instant afterward he saw a hand let something fall from the window. Don Felipe crossed the street rapidly and picked up what had been dropped. It was a note. He opened it immediately and read:

"Don Felipe, I cannot permit you to suffer without knowing my reasons. I also love you. Come to my house at ten in the morning. My parents will be at church."

At the appointed hour, Don Felipe went back to Marianita's house. She opened the door and pointed to a note on the table. It said:

"I am very unhappy. From birth I have been unable to speak. I am mute. Now you know the truth. But I must tell you that I love you very much."

—No, señor marqués —respondió Felipe—. Nunca he tenido la oportunidad. Pero creo que mis ojos le han hablado de mi amor y creo que Marianita lo ha comprendido.

El marqués luego dijo:

—Usted honra mi casa, pero hay un gran impedimento. Desde muy joven, mi hija tiene hecho un voto solemne de no casarse.

Felipe no pudo hablar. Sólo tenía la mirada fija en una de las paredes del salón de donde colgaba un precioso puñal de misericordia. (En tiempos antiguos los caballeros usaban estos puñales para matar a sus enemigos vencidos o para sacrificarse ellos mismos antes que ser humillados en la derrota.)

El joven sabía que bajo tal voto Marianita no cambiaría de opinión. Sin decir una palabra, don Felipe se levantó y se dirigió hacia la puerta. Lenta y tristemente, dijo al marqués:

—Me ha dejado usted muerto. Aquel puñal en la pared no podría haberlo hecho mejor.

—Lo siento mucho, don Felipe. Yo también sufro —contestó el marqués.

Don Felipe salió de la casa y cruzó la calle. Miró la casa como para decir adiós y creyó ver una cara en una de las ventanas. Un rayo de esperanza entró en su alma. No pudo moverse de ese lugar; e, instantes después, vio una mano que dejó caer algo por la ventana. Don Felipe cruzó la calle rápidamente y recogió lo que había caído. Era una nota. La abrió en seguida y leyó:

«Don Felipe, no puedo dejarlo sufrir sin que usted sepa mis razones. Yo también lo quiero. Venga a la casa mañana a las diez de la mañana. Mis padres estarán en la iglesia.»

A la hora indicada, don Felipe volvió a la casa de Marianita. Ella abrió la puerta e indicó con la mano una nota sobre la mesa que ella había escrito:

«Soy muy infeliz. Desde mi nacimiento no he podido hablar. Soy muda. Ahora sabes toda la verdad. Pero tengo que decirte que te quiero mucho.»

At that moment, Marianita reached for the dagger on the wall. She sank it deep into her throat. Marianita slowly fell to the floor, gazing at Felipe. Beside himself with horror, he ran to the door and screamed for help.

At that very moment, Marianita's parents arrived at the door. The marquis went for a doctor. Don Felipe bandaged the wound as best he could and asked Marianita, "Why did you do it? Why?"

After a while, the doctor arrived with Don Luis. He took care of Marianita and then said, "It's serious, but she will recover. In the meanwhile, she must have plenty of rest."

Marianita was still. She made a feeble sound, then another, a bit stronger. Looking at Don Felipe, she uttered these syllables, "Fe-li-pe."

Everyone was astounded. They could not believe it! Marianita herself was paralyzed with fear. Then she repeated the same syllables, "Fe-li-pe. Fe-li-pe."

Everyone exclaimed, "She can speak! She can speak!"

The surprised doctor explained that the dagger had probably cut some muscle or nerve that previously had impeded the use of her vocal cords.

Words could not express the happiness everyone felt at the time. They all cried tears of joy.

One month later, Marianita and Don Felipe were married. The couple was the most beautiful and happiest in the whole province. And in their home, on a prominent wall, hangs the mercy dagger.

Y en esos momentos, Marianita cogió el puñal de la pared. Lo hundió en su propia garganta. Marianita cayó lentamente al suelo, mirando a don Felipe. Él, fuera de sí, fue a la puerta y gritó:

—¡Socorro!

En ese momento llegaron a la puerta los padres de Marianita. El marqués fue por el médico. Don Felipe vendó la herida lo mejor que pudo a la vez que preguntaba a Marianita:

—¿Por qué has hecho esto? ¿Por qué?

Después de un rato llegó el médico con don Luis. Atendió a Marianita y luego les dijo:

—Es grave, pero se recuperará. Mientras tanto, ella necesita mucho descanso.

Marianita estaba inmóvil. Luego hizo un sonido, luego otro más fuerte. Y mirando a don Felipe, pronunció estas sílabas:

—Fe...li...pe.

Todos se quedaron atónitos. No podían creerlo. Marianita misma quedó paralizada de miedo. Luego repitió las mismas sílabas:

—Fe...li...pe. Fe...li...pe.

Y todos, a la vez, dijeron:

—¡Puede hablar! ¡Puede hablar!

El médico, sorprendido, explicó que a lo mejor la puñalada había cortado algún músculo o nervio que antes había impedido el uso de sus cuerdas vocales.

No se podría expresar con palabras la felicidad que todos sintieron en ese momento. Lloraban de alegría.

Un mes después, se celebró la boda de don Felipe y Marianita. No había en toda la comarca una pareja más hermosa ni más feliz. Y, en su casa, en una pared muy prominente, se puede ver colgado el puñal de misericordia.

15

The Mystery of the Lost Jewels

Spain has always produced beautiful works of art done in gold and silver. Spanish artisans are some of the finest in the world. Combining this art with that of gemstone cutting, they have produced jewelry recognized through the centuries for its exquisiteness and refinement. Their religious art is particularly outstanding.

El misterio de las joyas perdidas

España ha producido siempre hermosas obras de arte en oro y plata. Sus artesanos son unos de los mejores del mundo. Combinando este arte con el arte del tallado de piedras preciosas, han producido joyería que durante siglos ha sido reconocida por su exquisitez y refinamiento. Sobresalen particularmente en arte religioso.

*D*uring the reign of Phillip IV and Queen Isabel (1621–1665), everybody said that the women of the Spanish court were the most beautiful in the world. Among them was the Countess of la Peña. The Count of la Peña had fought in the Netherlands[1] and returned to Spain seriously wounded. After just one week, he died, leaving his wife a sad widow.

To forget her sadness, the countess requested permission of the queen to leave the court, intent on spending the rest of her days in solitude. The queen, naturally, granted her wish.

On taking leave of the countess, the queen removed from her breast a brooch of diamonds in the form of a cross and pinned it on the countess' dress, as a gift to her noble and unhappy friend.

The countess now lived in complete seclusion. Whenever she would leave her house, only her servant Catalina would accompany her.

Even though the countess had many valuable jewels, she no longer wore them, with the exception of her and her husband's wedding rings and the cross of diamonds given to her by the queen.

One day, as the countess returned to her quarters after breakfast, she removed the rings to wash her hands, and in a fit of forgetfulness, failed to put them back on. Some hours later she realized she was not wearing her rings and returned to the lavatory, which was next to a small window in her bedroom. She noticed that the ring engraved with her husband's name had disappeared.

She carefully searched everywhere she thought she might have left it. Finally she gave up.

She called Catalina and told her what had happened. Together they continued searching, but were unable to find it.

Two months later, other jewels disappeared, among them the precious cross of diamonds, the gift from the queen. The countess called Catalina, her only servant. She denied having taken it.

---

[1]Region that is currently equivalent to Holland, Belgium, and Luxembourg.

*D*urante el reinado de Felipe IV y la reina Isabel (1621–1665), se decía que las mujeres de la corte española eran las más bellas del mundo. Entre ellas estaba la condesa de la Peña. Su esposo, el conde de la Peña, había luchado en los Países Bajos[1] y volvió a España gravemente herido. Una semana más tarde, murió, dejando a su esposa viuda y triste.

Para poder olvidar su tristeza, la condesa pidió permiso a la reina para alejarse de la corte con el fin de pasar el resto de sus días en completa soledad. La reina, naturalmente, se lo concedió.

Al despedirse de la condesa, la reina se quitó del pecho un broche de brillantes en forma de cruz y lo prendió en el vestido de la condesa como recuerdo para su noble y desdichada amiga.

La condesa llevó una vida de absoluto retiro. Cuando salía de su casa, sólo la acompañaba su sirvienta, Catalina.

Aunque la condesa poseía muchas joyas valiosas, no las volvió a usar más, a excepción de las alianzas de ella y de su esposo y la cruz de brillantes, regalo de la reina.

Sucedió que cierto día, al regresar la condesa a sus habitaciones después de haber desayunado, se quitó los anillos para lavarse las manos y en inexplicable olvido, no se los volvió a poner. Unas horas más tarde, al darse cuenta, regresó a su lavatorio. Éste estaba junto a una pequeña ventana de su dormitorio. Notó con sorpresa que el anillo que tenía grabado el nombre de su esposo había desaparecido.

Buscó cuidadosamente en todos los lugares donde creía que podía haberlo dejado. Por fin, tuvo que darse por vencida.

Llamó a Catalina y le contó lo que había sucedido y juntas siguieron buscando sin poder encontrarlo.

Dos meses más tarde, otras joyas desaparecieron: entre ellas, la preciosa cruz de brillantes, regalo de la reina. La condesa llamó a Catalina, que era la única criada. Ella negó haberla tomado.

---

[1]Región que en la actualidad corresponde aproximadamente a los países de Holanda, Bélgica y Luxemburgo.

The poor girl, on bended knee and weeping profusely, claimed her innocence. But the countess did not believe her. The judge was notified and Catalina was jailed.

Several months went by. One day, some boys playing in the street in front of the countess' house heard a shrill shriek. When they turned to see where it had come from, they saw a crow perched on the roof of the house. It had something shiny in its beak. One of the boys picked up a stone and threw it with such strength and aim that it hit the bird right on the head. The crow immediately fell to the ground. All of them gathered around it, and one of the boys shouted, "Look, it's a crow and it has something in its beak!"

The bird had the precious jeweled cross! The boys, like all the townspeople, knew what had happened and they immediately picked up the crow, still with the cross in its beak, and took it to the countess. Seeing what the boys had brought her, she realized that the crow, and not Catalina, had stolen the cross. She fainted and, when she came to, said, "Catalina, Catalina, oh poor Catalina."

As soon as she could, the countess notified the judge that a crow had stolen the cross. The countess herself went to the jail to get Catalina. On her knees, the countess asked for forgiveness, "Catalina, I have wrongly accused you. I cannot live without your forgiveness."

"Madam," said Catalina, "you thought that was the right thing to do. Indeed, you don't know how much I have suffered, but I forgive you."

The countess took Catalina to her house.

Meanwhile, they found the crow's nest and were amazed to find the count's ring, other jewels, coins, and many other things that fascinate this kind of bird. It is well known that they have a tendency to pick up any object that shines and hide it in their nest.

The countess decided to give half her fortune to Catalina, and the two became very good friends.

La pobre muchacha, de rodillas y hecha un mar de lágrimas, juraba su inocencia. Pero la condesa no la creyó. Fue avisado el juez y la pobre Catalina fue encerrada en la cárcel.

Pasaron varios meses. Pero cierto día, unos muchachos, jugando en la calle frente a la casa de la condesa, oyeron un agudo chillido. Cuando miraron hacia donde venía el ruido, vieron un cuervo posado en el techo de la casa. Tenía algo brillante en el pico. Uno de los muchachos cogió una piedra y la tiró con tanta fuerza y puntería que dio precisamente en la cabeza del pobre pájaro y el cuervo cayó al suelo en el acto. Todos fueron a verlo y un muchacho gritó:

—¡Miren, es un cuervo y tiene algo en el pico!

¡El pájaro tenía la preciosa cruz de brillantes! Los muchachos, como todo habitante de la ciudad, sabían lo que había pasado antes y en seguida levantaron el cuervo, que todavía tenía la cruz en el pico, y lo llevaron a la condesa. Al ver lo que traían los muchachos, se dio cuenta de que el cuervo, y no Catalina, había robado la cruz. La condesa al instante se desmayó.

—Catalina, Catalina... pobre Catalina... —dijo al volver en sí.

La condesa, tan pronto como pudo, mandó avisar al juez que fue un cuervo el que robó la cruz. La condesa misma fue a la cárcel para sacar a Catalina. De rodillas, la condesa le pidió perdón:

—Catalina, yo te he acusado injustamente. No quiero vivir sin tu perdón.

—Señora —respondió Catalina—, usted creyó que eso era lo que tenía que hacer. De veras, no sabe usted lo mucho que he sufrido; pero le perdono.

La condesa llevó a Catalina a la casa.

Mientras tanto, encontraron el nido del cuervo, donde vieron, además del anillo del señor conde, otras alhajas, monedas y muchas otras cosas que provocan la fascinación de esta clase de ave. Es bien sabido que tienen la tendencia de llevarse y ocultar en sus nidos todo objeto que brilla.

La condesa decidió dar la mitad de su fortuna a Catalina y las dos llegaron a ser muy buenas amigas.

16

The Pirate's Cave

Majorca, the largest of the Balearic Islands,[1] is located two hundred kilometers from the east coast of Spain. Throughout their long history these islands have belonged to many countries,[2] but since the thirteenth century they have belonged to Spain.

The Majorcans are a mixture of several ancient Mediterranean tribes and they have always been good, gentle people. It is interesting to point out that toward the middle of the eighteenth century, a group of missionaries left Majorca for the New World. One of them, Father Junípero Serra, founded nine missions in California.

Continued on p. 96

La gruta del pirata

A doscientos kilómetros de la costa oriental de España está situada Mallorca, la más grande de las Islas Baleares.[1] A lo largo de su historia, estas islas han pertenecido a diferentes países,[2] pero desde el siglo XIII forman parte de España.

Los mallorquines son una mezcla de varias tribus primitivas del Mediterráneo, y siempre han sido gente humilde y buena. Es interesante notar que, a mediados del siglo XVIII, un grupo de misioneros salieron de Mallorca rumbo al Nuevo Mundo. Uno de ellos, el Padre Junípero Serra, fundó nueve misiones en la Alta California.

Continued on p. 97

---

[1]The Balearic Islands are Majorca, Menorca, Ibiza, Formentera, and Cabrera.
[2]The islands have belonged to the Carthaginians, Romans, Vandals, and Moors, among others.

[1]Las Islas Baleares son Mallorca, Menorca, Ibiza, Formentera y Cabrera.
[2]Las islas han pertenecido a los cartaginenses, a los romanos, a los vándalos y a los moros, entre otros.

For many centuries the Majorcans were victims of pirates, because piracy abounded in the Mediterranean Sea. In 1760, many pirates came from the north of Africa to the island of Majorca. Their favorite coasts were those on the southwest side, which had small bays where they could leave their boats while they robbed the people.

One day in autumn, the people of the little town of Artá were celebrating their harvest of fruit with a great feast. Suddenly, there came an invasion of pirates, shouting and waving their swords.

The pirates soon took the mayor captive and were carrying him away to their ship. But the people of the town fought so furiously that the pirates released their captive and ran to their ship. They swiftly left the island.

But not all of them left. There was a young pirate who, attempting to flee, fell on the rocks at the beach and broke his leg. With great difficulty, he dragged himself to a cave that was near the beach.

"Here I am going to wait for my companions to return," he said to himself. "They will come back soon to look for me. But first, I will bandage my leg because it hurts so much." So the brave and smart young man bandaged his leg with a piece of cloth from his turban. Then, since he was hungry, he decided to look for food. Fortunately, there were some shepherds who kept their goats in this cave. Subsisting on their milk, he was able to stay hidden in the cave for a few days.

The young pirate waited every day for the ship to come back for him. But his companions thought he was either dead or a prisoner, and didn't return.

One day, some fishermen from the town saw the young man seated at the entrance to the cave. Immediately, they took him to the mayor's house. Here the mayor's family helped him heal his wounds and gave him good food. He was always treated with respect and affection.

Durante varios siglos, los mallorquines fueron víctimas de los piratas, pues abundaba la piratería en el Mediterráneo. En el año 1760, eran muchos los piratas que navegaban del norte de África a la isla de Mallorca. Sus costas favoritas eran las del suroeste donde había muchas bahías pequeñas donde podían dejar sus barcos mientras robaban a los pobladores.

Un día de otoño, la gente del pequeño pueblo de Artá estaba celebrando su cosecha de fruta con una alegre fiesta. De repente, hubo una invasión de piratas, que venían gritando y blandiendo sus espadas.

Pronto los piratas hicieron prisionero al alcalde y lo llevaban hacia su barco. Sin embargo, la gente del pueblo peleó con tanta furia que los piratas soltaron a su cautivo y corrieron a su barco. Inmediatamente abandonaron la isla a toda velocidad.

Pero no todos se fueron. Hubo un joven pirata que, intentando huir, se cayó en las rocas de la playa y se rompió una pierna. Con gran dificultad se arrastró hasta una gran cueva cerca de la playa.

—Aquí voy a esperar la vuelta de mis compañeros —se decía a sí mismo—. Muy pronto volverán a buscarme. Pero primero voy a vendarme la pierna que tanto me duele—. Así el valeroso e inteligente joven se vendó la pierna con un pedazo de tela de su turbante. Entonces, como tenía hambre, decidió ir a buscar alimentos. Afortunadamente, había unos pastores que guardaban sus cabras en la cueva. Así, con la leche de estos animales, el joven pudo pasar unos días sin necesidad de salir.

Todos los días el joven esperaba ver su barco en el mar. Pero sus compañeros, creyéndolo muerto o prisionero, nunca volvieron.

Un día los pescadores del pueblo vieron al joven sentado frente a la cueva. En seguida lo llevaron a la casa del buen alcalde. Aquí toda la familia le ayudó a curar sus heridas y le dieron buena comida. Siempre fue tratado con respeto y cariño.

Gradually, the young man forgot his hatred for his companions who had so cruelly abandoned him. He offered himself as a servant to the mayor who had treated him so kindly.

"I happily accept your help. But now you are a beloved member of our family," said the mayor.

The young man worked faithfully for many months. In this way he gained the respect and affection of the whole town and the love of the mayor's family. The young man eventually fell in love with the mayor's daughter and, after a year, they were married and happily lived the rest of their lives in the town near the Pirate's Cave.

Poco a poco, el joven olvidó su odio hacia sus compañeros que tan cruelmente lo habían abandonado. Se ofreció como criado al alcalde que lo había tratado con tanta amabilidad.

—Con mucho gusto acepto tu ayuda. Pero ahora eres un querido miembro de nuestra familia —dijo el alcalde.

El joven trabajó fielmente durante muchos meses. Así ganó el respeto y el cariño de todo el pueblo y el amor de la familia del alcalde. La verdad es que el joven se enamoró de la hija del alcalde y después de un año se casaron y vivieron felices toda su vida en el pueblo, cerca de la Gruta del Pirata.

17

The Spirits

During the years of colonization of the New World, hundreds of thousands of Spaniards attempted to make their fortunes in America, known at the time as The Indies.[1] The tales of gold and silver attracted many of them. Many Spaniards became wealthy and returned to Spain with their fortunes. Those who came from The Indies were called *indianos*. This legend has to do with a wealthy *indiano* who arrives in Andalusia.

Las ánimas

En los años de la colonización del Nuevo Mundo, cientos de miles de españoles trataron de hacer fortuna en América, conocida como Indias[1] en ese tiempo. Las leyendas del oro y la plata atrajeron a muchos. Había veces en que estos españoles se hacían ricos y volvían a España con sus fortunas. A éstos se les llamaba "indianos" porque venían de las Indias. La siguiente leyenda tiene que ver con un rico indiano llegado a Andalucía.

---

[1]The first explorers who arrived in America did not know they had encountered a new continent. They thought they had reached southeastern Asia, which at the time was known as The Indies.

[1]Los primeros exploradores que llegaron a las Américas no sabían que habían encontrado un continente nuevo. Creían que habían llegado al sudeste de Asia, que se conocía como las Indias en aquella época.

*A*round the south of Spain, in Andalusia, there was once an elderly woman who had a beautiful and good niece who also happened to be very lazy. The elderly woman was desperate for her to get married. She was afraid she would die and leave her poor niece without a husband.

It so happened that an *indiano* came to the town where the aunt and the niece lived. He was good-looking, rich, and in search of a wife. The aunt immediately went to the gentleman, saying she had a niece who possessed so many talents that no book could list them all. The gentleman said that he would very much like to meet her and that the next day he would go to the house to visit her.

The following day, the gentleman arrived and asked, "Does your niece know how to spin?"

"Does she know how to spin?" replied the aunt. "That is precisely what gives her the most pleasure."

The gentleman went away very happy. After a while, many servants arrived at the house, loaded down with skeins of fine linen. The head servant said to the aunt, "My master asks that by tomorrow all this be spun."

The niece, hearing this, cried bitterly because she didn't know how to spin; she had never spun in her life.

"What am I going to do? What am I going to do?" she repeated. "I want to marry that *indiano*. What am I going to do?" she continued crying.

At that moment, three spirits dressed in white appeared to her. They were good and kind spirits, and soon began to spin the linen. In no time, all the skeins had been spun into very fine thread. Then the spirits disappeared.

The following morning, when the aunt saw the miracle, she could hardly contain her joy. When the rich *indiano* arrived, he congratulated his fiancée on her ability. But then it occurred to him to ask her if she knew how to sew.

"You ask if she knows how to sew?" the aunt hurriedly said. "Sewing is her delight and she does it very rapidly."

The *indiano* left, very happy, and in a short while the servants arrived, loaded down with bolts of linen cloth.

Se cuenta que por el sur de España, en Andalucía, había una vez una viejita que tenía una sobrina linda y buena, pero muy perezosa. Se desesperaba la vieja al no poder casarla. Temía morir y dejar a la pobre sobrina sin esposo.

Sucedió que llegó al pueblo en donde vivían la tía y la sobrina un indiano muy rico y guapo que quería casarse. La tía fue inmediatamente al caballero diciendo que ella tenía una sobrina cuyos talentos eran tantos que no bastaría un libro para contarlos. El caballero le contestó que le gustaría mucho conocerla y así él iría al día siguiente a su casa a visitarla.

Al día siguiente llegó el caballero y preguntó:

—¿Sabe su sobrina hilar?

—¿Cómo, hilar? —dijo la tía—. Si precisamente ése es el mayor gusto de ella.

El caballero se fue muy contento. Al poco rato empezaron a llegar a la casa de la tía muchos criados cargados con madejas de lino. Decía el jefe de los criados:

—Dice mi señor que para mañana todo debe estar hilado.

La muchacha, al oír esto, se puso a llorar amargamente porque ella no sabía hilar; nunca había hilado.

—¿Qué voy a hacer? ¿Qué voy a hacer? —repetía ella—. Yo quiero casarme con el indiano. ¿Qué voy a hacer? —Y seguía llorando.

En ese instante aparecieron, vestidas de blanco, tres ánimas, de las buenas, y se pusieron a hilar. En poco tiempo convirtieron todas las madejas de lino en hilo fino. Luego desaparecieron.

Cuando a la mañana siguiente la tía vio aquel milagro, apenas pudo contenerse de la alegría. Y cuando llegó el rico caballero indiano, felicitó a su novia por su habilidad. Pero entonces se le ocurrió preguntarle si sabía coser.

—¿Si sabe ella coser? —se apresuró a decir la tía—. Coser es un placer para ella y lo hace con mucha rapidez.

El indiano se fue muy contento y al poco rato empezaron a llegar criados y más criados cargados de piezas de lienzo.

"My master says the young lady should make jackets and shirts out of this for him," the head servant said.

Once more the girl, who knew nothing about cutting or sewing, began to cry.

The three spirits appeared again, and in just a short while had cut all the linen and had made jackets and shirts. Then they disappeared.

The girl's aunt danced with joy and the *indiano* could not stop congratulating himself for having found such a talented fiancée.

Then it occurred to the *indiano* to send the girl dozens of vests.

"My master wants them all embroidered, all different and in every color," said the head servant.

The girl, even sadder than before, cried bitterly again.

As on the previous occasions, the three spirits appeared and in a short while had all the vests embroidered.

"We've done all this work with pleasure," the spirits said, "but all we ask is to be invited to the wedding banquet."

"Why, of course!" agreed the girl.

When the *indiano* saw the vests so finely embroidered in such a short time, he didn't doubt one instant that he had found the most capable fiancée in all of Spain. He was determined not to let this treasure escape. He wanted to marry her immediately.

The girl was sad because by this time she was truly in love with the *indiano*. He was good and handsome. But she knew he would eventually realize she was not the capable person he thought she was.

The wedding day arrived. The banquet was splendid and the guests were very happy, eating, laughing, and dancing. Among the guests who arrived late were three old, ugly women. They were so ugly that everyone stopped eating, laughing, and dancing to look at them, their mouths wide open. One of the old ladies had one very short arm and one that was very long. Another was hunchbacked and had a twisted body. And the third one had red, bulging eyes.

—Dice mi señor que la señorita debe hacer con esto chaquetas y camisas para él —dijo el jefe de los criados.

Otra vez la muchacha, que no sabía nada de cortar ni coser,
se puso a llorar.

Las tres ánimas volvieron a aparecer y en poco tiempo
habían cortado todo el lienzo y habían hecho las chaquetas y
camisas. Luego desaparecieron.

La tía de la muchacha bailaba de gusto y el indiano no
cesaba de congratularse por tener una novia tan lista.

Pero entonces se le ocurrió al indiano enviarle a la muchacha
docenas de chalecos.

—Dice mi señor que los quiere bordados, todos diferentes y
de todos los colores —decía el jefe de los criados.

La muchacha, cada vez más triste, comenzó a llorar amargamente otra vez.

Como en las otras ocasiones, las tres ánimas aparecieron y en
poco tiempo tenían todos los chalecos bordados.

—Con gusto hemos hecho todo este trabajo —decían las
ánimas—, pero lo único que pedimos es que nos invites al banquete de tu boda.

—¡Pero, cómo no! —contestó la muchacha.

Cuando el indiano vio los chalecos bordados y en tan poco
tiempo, no dudó un instante que tenía la novia más capaz de
toda España y estaba resuelto a no dejar escapar aquel tesoro. Él
quería casarse al instante.

La muchacha estaba muy triste porque se había enamorado
ya del indiano. Era muy guapo y bueno. Pero ella sabía que él se
daría cuenta de que ella no era trabajadora y que no sabía hacer
nada.

Llegó el día de la boda. El banquete era espléndido y todos
los convidados estaban muy contentos, comiendo, riendo y bai-
lando. Entre los convidados que llegaron tarde, había tres viejecitas tan feas que todos dejaron de comer, de reírse y de bailar,
mirándolas con la boca abierta. Una de ellas tenía un brazo muy
corto y el otro larguísimo; otra era jorobada con el cuerpo torcido; y la tercera tenía los ojos saltones y colorados.

When the girl realized that the three old women were the three spirits, she said to her husband, "These are three very special aunts of mine."

"Well, since you have invited them, my dear wife, they are very welcome."

And he went to talk to them very kindly and offered them a seat.

Since the three old women were very talkative, they took part in every conversation. Finally, one of the guests, unable to contain himself, asked one of the women why she had one short arm and one long one.

"My son," responded the woman in a high-pitched voice, "my arms are that way because I spin so much."

Hearing this, the groom looked at his wife's beautiful white, round arms and said to her, "I don't want you to spin ever again."

Another guest asked the second woman why her eyes were bulging and red.

"I have spent my entire life cutting and sewing."

The groom then whispered to his wife, "I don't want you to cut or sew either."

Then another guest asked the third woman why she was hunchbacked and why her body was so twisted.

"Oh, my son!" the old woman said. "I'm that way from bending over so much while doing embroidery."

The groom again whispered to his bride, "I don't want you to embroider anymore either."

And the three old women, who in reality were the three spirits, disappeared, and the gentleman and his wife were very happy together.

Cuando la muchacha se dio cuenta de que las tres viejecitas eran las tres ánimas, dijo a su marido:

—Son tres tías muy queridas...

—Pues tú las has convidado, mi querida esposa; sean bienvenidas.

Y él fue a hablarles con mucho cariño y a ofrecerles asiento.

Como eran muy conversadoras, las viejitas en seguida se pusieron a charlar con los demás. Al fin, un convidado curioso no pudo resistirlo y preguntó a la primera cómo era que tenía un brazo corto siendo el otro tan largo.

—Hijo mío —dijo la vieja en voz muy alta—, los tengo así por lo mucho que he hilado.

El novio, oyendo esto y que en aquel instante contemplaba los brazos de su mujer, tan blancos y redondos, se le acercó a ella y le dijo:

—No debes hilar más en tu vida.

Mientras tanto, otro convidado preguntaba a la segunda viejita por qué tenía los ojos tan saltones y colorados.

—He pasado la vida cortando y cosiendo.

El novio dijo al oído de su esposa:

—Tampoco debes cortar ni coser.

Más tarde, otro curioso preguntaba a la tercera viejita cómo era que tenía la espalda jorobada y el cuerpo tan torcido.

—¡Ay, hijo mío! —contestó la viejita—. Estoy así de tanto inclinarme para bordar.

El novio, hablándole otra vez a su esposa, dijo:

—No debes bordar más en tu vida.

Y las viejitas, que eran las ánimas, desaparecieron; y el caballero y su esposa fueron muy felices.

18

The Lady of Stone

In the north of Spain, not far from the Basque city of Oyarzún, in open country, there was a small chapel dedicated to St. James the Apostle.[1] The chapel was neither luxurious nor richly adorned. The chapel's fame was not based on its dedication to St. James the Apostle, but rather on a rosary that the statue of the Virgin Mary had in her hands.

Truly, the rosary was marvelous, and everyone said that it was the most beautiful in the world.

La dama de piedra

En el norte de España, no muy lejos de la ciudad vascongada de Oyarzún, en pleno campo, había una pequeña capilla dedicada al Apóstol Santiago.[1] La capilla no era nada lujosa ni tampoco estaba ricamente adornada. Era muy conocida, sin embargo, no por estar dedicada a Santiago, sino por un rosario que tenía en sus manos una estatua de la Virgen.

En verdad, era una maravilla el rosario y decían todos que no había otro de igual hermosura en todo el mundo.

---

[1]St. James is the patron saint of Spain. It is believed that his remains rest in the city of Santiago de Compostela. Thus there is a famous pilgrimage route known as the *Camino de Santiago* (James's Road).

[1]Santiago es el santo patrón de España. Se cree que sus restos reposan en la ciudad de Santiago de Compostela. De ahí la famosa ruta de peregrinación conocida como el Camino de Santiago.

On one occasion, a group of people on horseback passed near the chapel of Oyarzún. Among these people, there was a French lady of high noble birth. A young Frenchman served as a guide for the group. As they rode along, he and the lady were chatting and laughing to take their minds off the inconveniences and weariness of their trip. Suddenly the lady saw a chapel among the trees and shouted to the young man, "Look, a chapel! Let's go, you and I, and enter the chapel to rest a bit. I cannot go any farther. I'm so tired."

This surprised the young man, for he knew that the lady had little faith in God and little respect for religion. But since he too was tired and wanted to escape the Spanish heat, he agreed.

He ordered everyone to stop. Then both of them headed toward the chapel and entered into the darkness.

"Oh, how tired I am," exclaimed the lady. "How very cool it is in here."

"Yes," said the young man. "It is a good place to rest. But it is so dark!"

After a while the lady's eyes became accustomed to the darkness of the chapel and she noticed the rosary in the hands of the statue of the Virgin.

"What beautiful jewels!" the lady exclaimed. "They are the prettiest I have ever seen in my whole life. I must have them! Do you understand? Get them for me!"

"My lady," the young man said, "these jewels are sacred. You don't really want them. You can have any jeweler make you a rosary much prettier than this one. Forgive me, but you don't know what you're asking me to do."

"You're afraid, aren't you?" answered the lady. "You are a gentleman and you are afraid. If you don't get the rosary for me—sacred or not—I'll get it myself."

In a flash, before the astonished eyes of the young man, she went up to the altar where the statue of the Virgin was, grabbed the rosary, and hid it in a little pocket of her skirt. Not the least ashamed, she left the chapel, followed by the young man. He could not believe what he had just witnessed. The lady got on her horse and set out toward the other travelers. The young man did the same.

En una ocasión, pasó cerca de esta capilla de Oyarzún un grupo de gente a caballo. Entre ellos, había una señora francesa de alta nobleza. Un joven caballero francés servía de guía al grupo. Él y la dama, mientras caminaban, charlaban y se reían para distraerse de las incomodidades y el cansancio del viaje. De repente, la dama vio entre los árboles una capilla y gritó al joven:

—¡Mira, ahí hay una capilla! Vamos tú y yo y entremos a descansar un rato. No puedo seguir más; estoy cansadísima.

Esto le extrañó un poco al caballero porque sabía que la dama era persona de poca fe y respeto religioso. Pero, como él también estaba cansado y quería escapar del calor español, asintió.

Ordenando a toda la gente a que se parara, los dos se dirigieron a la capilla y entraron en la oscuridad de su interior.

—¡Ay, cómo estoy cansada! —dijo la dama—. ¡Y qué fresco está aquí adentro!

—Sí —dijo el caballero—, sí es buen lugar para descansar. ¡Pero está muy oscuro!

Después de un rato, los ojos de la dama se acostumbraron a la poca luz que había en la capilla y se fijaron en el rosario que estaba en las manos de la estatua de la Virgen.

—¡Qué bonitas joyas! —exclamó la dama—. Son las más hermosas que he visto en mi vida. Tienen que ser mías, ¿entiendes? ¡Cógemelas!

—Señora —contestó el caballero—, estas joyas son sagradas. ¿Por qué las quiere? Si usted puede mandar a cualquier joyero que le haga un rosario mucho más bonito que éste. Perdone, pero usted no sabe lo que me está pidiendo.

—Tienes miedo, ¿no? —respondió la dama—. Tú, el caballero... y tienes miedo. Si no me das el rosario, sagrado o no, yo misma lo voy a coger.

Y en el acto, ante los ojos atónitos del caballero, subió al altar donde estaba la estatua de la Virgen, cogió el rosario y lo escondió en un bolsillo de su falda. Sin la más mínima vergüenza, salió de la capilla seguida por el caballero. Él no podía creer lo que acababa de ver. La dama montó en su caballo y se dirigió hacia los otros viajeros. El caballero hizo lo mismo.

He felt guilty for having allowed the theft in the chapel. He no longer wanted to talk. But the lady, once the group resumed their journey, began to talk and laugh as she had previously. What was worse, she actually seemed proud of what she had done.

Along the way, a poorly dressed old man approached them. When he was directly in front of the lady and the travelers, he shouted in a deep, serious voice, "Travelers, stop!"

Although the old man hardly inspired fear, some of the men drew their swords.

The old man was not silent and in a loud voice, he addressed the men in the group. "I ask nothing of you, nothing at all. It's the lady with whom I must speak."

And then, turning to the lady he added, "I ask you, Madam, to return the rosary that you have just stolen from the Virgin."

The lady grew pale, more from anger than from fear, and arrogantly denied the theft.

"What is this old man saying? I have not stolen anything from anybody. This old man is crazy. He doesn't know what he is talking about."

But the old man replied, "I know you stole that rosary."

She was beside herself with rage, and she blurted, "May I turn to stone if what I say is not the truth!"

The moment she spoke those words, the lady turned to stone.

Even today, one can see a slab of stone with the figure of a woman on horseback near the chapel.

Él se reprochaba interiormente su falta de valor al haber consentido el robo de la capilla. No quiso hablar. Pero la dama, una vez que todos se pusieron en marcha, empezó la conversación tan alegre como antes. Hasta estaba orgullosa de lo que había hecho.

En el camino, llegando hacia ellos, apareció un viejecillo vestido muy pobremente. Al llegar ante la dama y los otros viajeros, gritó con voz grave y profunda:

—¡Alto a los caminantes!

A pesar de que la figura del viejo no podía inspirar miedo, algunos de los hombres del grupo sacaron sus espadas.

El anciano no se calló, sino que habló con voz fuerte a los señores del grupo:

—De ustedes no pido nada, absolutamente nada. Es con la señora con quien tengo que hablar.

Y luego, volviéndose a la dama, añadió:

—Le pido a usted, señora, que devuelva el rosario que acaba de robar a la Virgen.

La dama se puso pálida, más de ira que de miedo, y negó el robo con soberbia.

—¿Qué dice este hombre? No he robado nada a nadie. Este viejo está loco. No sabe lo que dice.

Pero el viejito respondió:

—Yo sé que es usted quien ha robado ese rosario.

Pero ella, furiosa y fuera de sí, exclamó:

—¡Que me convierta en piedra si no es verdad lo que digo!

Y, al momento de pronunciar estas palabras, la dama se convirtió en roca.

Todavía hoy, puede verse una lápida con la figura de una mujer a caballo cerca de la capilla.

English-Spanish Vocabulary
Vocabulario inglés-español

All words that appear in the text are included here, except for exact or very close cognates, definite articles, some pronouns, cardinal numbers, and names of people, places, months, and days.

The following abbreviations are used:

abbrev., abbreviation
adj., adjective
adv., adverb
art., article
conj., conjunction
dim., diminutive
f., feminine
irreg., irregular
m., masculine
n., noun

obj., object
p.p., past participle
pl., plural
poss., possessive
prep., preposition
pres. p., present participle
pron., pronoun
sing., singular
v., verb

A

a *(indefinite art.)* un, una; **an** *(in place of* **a** *before a word beginning with a vowel sound)*
abandon *(v.)* abandonar
ability habilidad, capacidad
able capaz; **to be able to** poder, ser capaz (de)
abound *(v.)* abundar
about *(prep.)* acerca de, sobre; *(adv.)* aproximadamente, cerca de; **to be about to** estar por
absolutely *(adv.)* absolutamente
accept *(v.)* aceptar
accompany *(v.)* acompañar
accomplish *(v.)* realizar, lograr, cumplir
according to *(prep.)* de acuerdo con, según
accuse *(v.)* acusar; **accused** *(p.p. & adj.)* acusado, -a

accustom *(v.)* acostumbrar, habituar; **to grow accustomed** acostumbrarse, habituarse
acknowledge *(v.)* reconocer, admitir
acknowledgment reconocimiento, admisión
act *(n.)* acto; *(v.)* actuar, proceder
actually *(adv.)* en realidad, en verdad
add *(v.)* sumar, agregar, añadir
addition *(n.)* suma, adición; **in addition** *(adv.)* además
address *(n.)* dirección; *(v.)* dirigirse a *(una persona)*; dirigir *(una correspondencia)* a alguien
adjacent *(adj.)* adyacente
adjective adjetivo
admire *(v.)* admirar; **admirer** *(n.)* admirador, -a
admit *(v.)* admitir, confesar
adopt *(v.)* adoptar

adorn *(v.)* adornar, decorar;
  adorned *(p.p. & adj.)*
  adornado, -a; decorado, -a
advance *(n.)* avance, adelanto *(m.)*;
  (v.) avanzar, adelantar(se)
adventure aventura
advice *(n.)* consejo, advertencia
advise *(v.)* aconsejar, advertir
affair asunto, caso, cuestión; **affairs**
  negocios
affection afecto, cariño
affectionately *(adv.)*
  afectuosamente, cariñosamente
afraid; to be afraid of tener miedo
  de, temer (a)
after *(prep. & conj.)* después (de),
  tras; *(adv.)* siguiente
afternoon tarde *(f.)*, atardecer *(m.)*
afterward *(adv.)* después, luego
again *(adv.)* otra vez, de nuevo,
  nuevamente; **once again** una vez
  más, otra vez
against *(prep.)* contra
age edad *(f.)*, época; **Middle Ages**
  Edad Media
agitated *(p.p. & adj.)* agitado, -a
ago *(adj. & adv.)* atrás *(en el
  tiempo)*; *(expression of time)* +
  ago hace + *(expression of time)*
agony agonía
agreed *(p.p. & adj.)* acordado, -a
aid *(n.)* ayuda, socorro, auxilio;
  (v.) ayudar, socorrer, auxiliar
aim *(n.)* objetivo, meta, puntería;
  (v.) apuntar, ponerse por meta
air aire
alarmed *(p.p. & adj.)* alarmado, -a
alive *(adj. & adv.)* vivo, -a; con vida
all *(adj.)* todo, -a; todos, -as; *(pron.)*
  todo; todos, -as
Allah Alá *(m.)*
almost *(adv.)* casi
alone *(adj.)* solo, -a; solitario, -a
along *(prep.)* a lo largo de
already *(adv.)* ya
also *(adv.)* también, además

although *(conj.)* aunque, a pesar de
  (que)
always *(adv.)* siempre
am *(present tense)* soy, estoy;
  (infinitive) **to be**
amaze *(v.)* pasmar, sorprender,
  admirar; **amazed** *(p.p. & adj.)*
  pasmado, -a; sorprendido, -a;
  admirado, -a
ambush *(v.)* emboscar; **ambushed**
  (p.p. & adj.) emboscado, -a;
  agazapado, -a
among *(prep.)* entre, de entre
an *(indefinite art.)* *(used in place of* **a**
  *before a word beginning with a
  vowel sound)*
ancient *(adj.)* antiguo, -a
and y, e *(in place of* y *before a word
  beginning with* i *or* hi*)*
anger ira, rabia, enojo, enfado
another *(adj. & pron.)* otro, -a
answer *(n.)* respuesta, contestación;
  (v.) responder, contestar
anticipate *(v.)* anticipar
anxious *(adj.)* ansioso; **anxiously**
  (adv.) ansiosamente
any *(adj. & pron.)* cualquier, -a;
  ninguno (ningún), -a
anybody (=**anyone**) *(pron.)*
  cualquier persona; cualquier, -a;
  nadie; ninguno (ningún), -a
anymore *(adv.)* ya no, no… más
anyone (=**anybody**) *(pron.)*
  cualquier persona; cualquier, -a
anything *(pron.)* cualquier cosa,
  nada
apart *(adj.)* separado, -a; aparte
apostle apóstol
appear *(v.)* aparecer, parecer
appoint *(v.)* designar, nombrar,
  elegir
appreciate *(v.)* apreciar
approach *(v.)* acercar(se),
  aproximar(se)
appropriate *(adj.)* apropiado, -a
approve *(v.)* aprobar

apron delantal

Arabian (adj.) árabe (m. & f.); (n.) árabe, nativo o habitante de Arabia

Arabic (adj.) árabe

arch arco

archbishop arzobispo

architect arquitecto, -a

are (present tense) son, están; (infinitive) to be

aren't (are + not) no son, no están; there aren't (pl.) no hay

arise (v.) levantarse; arose (past tense) se levantó

arm (n.) brazo, arma; (v.) armar(se); (p.p. & adj.) armado, -a

armor armadura

arose (past tense) se levantó; (infinitive) to arise

around (prep.) alrededor de; (adv.) alrededor; hover around rondar

arrange (v.) arreglar, hacer arreglos, disponer, buscar cómo

arrangement (v.) arreglo, acuerdo, disposición

arrival llegada

arrive (v.) llegar

arrogantly (adv.) arrogantemente, con arrogancia

arrow flecha

art arte

artisan artesano, -a

artist artista (m. & f.)

as (conj.) como, mientras, a medida que; as . . . as tan… como; as if como si

as luck would have it por esas cosas del destino

ask (v.) preguntar, hacer una pregunta; ask for pedir

ashamed (p.p. & adj.) avergonzado, -a; not the least ashamed sin la más mínima vergüenza

asleep (adj. & adv.) dormido, -a; fall asleep dormirse

assassin asesino, -a

assume (v.) asumir, suponer, presuponer; assumed (p.p. & adj.) asumido, -a; supuesto, -a; presupuesto, -a

assure (v.) asegurar, garantizar; assured (p.p. & adj.) asegurado, -a; garantizado, -a

astonished (p.p. & adj.) atónito, -a; pasmado, -a; admirado, -a

astounded (p.p. & adj.) atónito, -a; pasmado, -a; admirado, -a

at (prep.) a, en; at once en el acto, al instante; at times a veces; look at mirar

ate (past tense) comió; (infinitive) to eat

attempt (v.) intentar, tratar (de), probar

attend (to) (v.) asistir, atender

attentively (adv.) atenciosamente, con atención, con cuidado

attitude actitud

attract (v.) atraer

aunt tía

authenticity autenticidad

autumn otoño

avoid (v.) evitar

await (v.) aguardar, esperar

awe admiración, pasmo; in awe maravillado, -a; pasmado, -a; admirado, -a; sorprendido, -a

awake (v.) despertarse; awoke (past tense) se despertó

B

back (adv.) de vuelta, de nuevo, otra vez

back (n.) espalda; with one's back to (something) de espaldas a

bad (adj.) malo (mal), -a

bag bolsa, saco

baker panadero, pastelero

balcony balcón

Balearic Islands Islas Baleares

bandage *(n.)* vendaje *(m.); (v.)* vendar

bank orilla, banco *(de una masa de agua)*

base *(v.)* basar(se); **based** *(p.p. & adj.)* basado, -a

Basque *(adj. & n.)* vasco, -a; vascongado, -a; *(n.)* lengua vasca

bath baño

bathe *(v.)* bañarse

battle batalla

bay bahía

be *(v.)* ser, estar; *(present tense)* **am** soy, estoy; **are** son, están; **is** es, está; *(past tense)* **was** era, estaba, fue, estuvo; **were** eran, estaban, fueron, estuvieron; *(p.p.)* **been** sido, estado

be located estar ubicado, -a; estar situado, -a

beach playa

beak pico *(de ave)*

beautiful hermoso, lindo, bello

beauty hermosura, belleza

became *(past tense)* llegó a ser, se volvió, se convirtió; *(infinitive)* **to become**

because *(conj.)* porque, ya que, pues

become *(v.)* llegar a ser, volverse, convertirse; **became** *(past tense)* llegó a ser, se volvió, se convirtió; **become dark** oscurecerse

bed cama

bedroom dormitorio, cuarto, habitación

bedside lado de la cama; **from his bedside** desde su lecho, desde su cama

been *(p.p.)* sido, estado; *(infinitive)* **to be**

before *(prep.)* antes (de); *(adv.)* antes; *(conj.)* antes, antes de, antes (de) que

before *(prep.)* ante, frente a, en presencia de

beg *(v.)* rogar, suplicar, implorar; **begged** *(past tense)* rogó, suplicó, imploró

began *(past tense)* comenzó, empezó; *(infinitive)* **to begin**

begged *(past tense)* rogó, suplicó, imploró; *(infinitive)* **to beg**

begin *(v.)* comenzar, empezar; **began** *(past tense)* comenzó, empezó

beginning *(pres. p.)* comenzando, empezando; *(infinitive)* **to begin**

beginning *(n.)* principio; **in the beginning, at the beginning** en el principio, a principios

behind *(prep.)* detrás (de), atrás (de); *(adv.)* detrás, atrás

being *(pres. p.)* siendo, estando; *(infinitive)* **to be**

being *(n.)* ser *(m.)*

believe *(v.)* creer, pensar; **are believed to (be)** se cree que (son)

bell campana

belong (to) *(v.)* pertenecer (a)

beloved *(adj.)* amado, -a; querido, -a

bend *(v.)* doblar, curvar, torcer; **on bended knee** de rodillas

bent *(p.p. & adj.)* doblado, curvado, torcido; *(infinitive)* **to bend**

beside *(prep.)* al lado de; **beside oneself** fuera de sí

besides *(adv.)* además; *(prep.)* además de

best *(superlative adj.)* (el, la) mejor; *(pron.)* el, la mejor; *(adv.)* mejor

bestow (on) *(v.)* brindar, dar

Bethlehem Belén

betrayal traición *(f.)*

betray *(v.)* traicionar

better *(comparative adj.)* mejor; **better than** mejor que, más bueno que

between *(prep.)* entre

big grande (gran) *(m. & f.)*

bird ave, pájaro

birth nacimiento
bit *(n.)* poco, algo; **a (little) bit** un poco
bitterly *(adv.)* amargamente
black *(adj.)* negro, -a
blame *(v.)* culpar, acusar
bleed *(v.)* sangrar; **bleeding** *(pres. p. & adj.)* sangriento
bless *(v.)* bendecir; **blessed** *(p.p. & adj.)* bendecido, -a; bendito, -a
blessing *(n.)* bendición *(f.)*
blood sangre
bloody sangriento, -a; ensangrentado, -a
blouse blusa
blurt (out) *(v.)* pronunciar abrupta e impulsivamente
boar jabalí; **wild boar** jabalí salvaje
boat barco
body cuerpo
bolt pieza de tela
book libro
born *(p.p. & adj.)* nacido, -a; **be born** nacer
both *(adj. & pron.)* ambos
bother *(v.)* molestar, incomodar, fastidiar
bought *(past tense)* compró, compraba; *(p.p. & adj.)* comprado, -a
bound (for) rumbo a
bouquet ramillete, buqué
box caja
boy niño
brave *(adj.)* valeroso, -a; valiente *(m. & f.)*; **bravest** *(superlative)* el, la más valeroso, -a; valerosísimo, -a
bravery *(n.)* valor *(m.)*, valentía, coraje *(m.)*
bread pan
break *(v.)* romper; **broke** *(past tense)* rompió, rompía; **broken** *(p.p. & adj.)* roto, -a
breakfast desayuno

breast pecho
breathlessly *(adv.)* sin aliento, jadeando
bride novia
bridge puente
bridle brida
bright *(adj.)* brillante *(m. & f.)*; luminoso, -a; claro, -a
brilliant *(adj.)* brillante *(m. & f.)*; luminoso, -a
bring *(v.)* llevar; **brought** *(past tense)* llevó, llevaba; *(p.p.)* llevado
broke *(past tense)* rompió, rompía; *(infinitive)* **to break**
broken *(p.p. & adj.)* roto, -a; *(infinitive)* **to break**
brooch broche *(m.)*
brother hermano
brought *(p.p.)* llevado; *(infinitive)* **to bring**
build *(v.)* construir, edificar; **built** *(past tense)* construyó, construía; *(p.p.)* construido
bulging *(adj.)* saltón, -a
bunch conjunto, grupo, mazo
bundle bulto
buried *(past tense)* enterró; *(p.p. & adj.)* enterrado, -a; *(infinitive)* **to bury**
burn *(v.)* quemar(se), incendiar(se); **burned** or **burnt** *(past tense)* (se) quemó, (se) quemaba; *(p.p. & adj.)* quemado, -a
bury *(v.)* enterrar; **buried** *(past tense)* enterró; *(p.p. & adj.)* enterrado, -a
businessman *(sing.)* hombre de negocios; **businessmen** *(pl.)* hombres de negocios
but *(conj.)* pero; **nothing . . . but** sino
butter mantequilla
buy *(v.)* comprar
by *(prep.)* por, cerca de, junto a; **go by, pass by** pasar

C

calculation cálculo

call (v.) llamar(se), clamar

came (past tense) vino, venía; (infinitive) to come

camp (n.) campamento

can (v.) poder, ser capaz de; cannot, can't (can + not) no puede, no es capaz de; could (past tense) pudo, podía

candle vela

candlestick candelero

candy dulce, caramelo

cannot (can + not) no puede, no es capaz de; (pres. tense) can

canvas lienzo (de pintura)

capable (adj.) capaz (m. & f.)

cape capa

captain capitán, -ana

captive cautivo, -a

capture (v.) capturar

care (n.) cuidado, atención; take care of, care for cuidar, atender

carefully (adv.) cuidadosamente

caress (n.) caricia; (v.) acariciar

carpenter carpintero

carry (v.) llevar, cargar, portar; carried (past tense) llevó, llevaba; (p.p.) llevado

case caso

Castilian castellano

castle castillo

cat gato

cathedral catedral

cause (n.) causa; (v.) causar

cave cueva, gruta

celebrate (v.) celebrar

century siglo, centuria; centuries (pl.)

ceremony ceremonia

certain (adj.) cierto, -a; dado, -a

change (n.) cambio; (v.) cambiar

chapel capilla

character personaje (m.), personalidad, carácter (m.)

chase (n.) perseguimiento, persecución; (v.) perseguir, dar caza a

chat (n.) charla, conversación, tertulia; (v.) charlar, conversar; chatted (past tense) charló, charlaba; (p.p.) charlado

cheek mejilla

chest pecho

chief jefe, -a

child (sing.) niño, -a; hijo, -a; children (pl.)

childhood niñez (f.)

choice elección, selección

Christian (adj. & n.) cristiano, -a

Christmas Navidad (f.)

Christopher Columbus Cristóbal Colón

church iglesia

cite (v.) citar

city ciudad (f.); cities (pl.)

claim (n.) reclamo, aseveración; (v.) clamar, reclamar, aseverar, afirmar

clash choque (m.)

class clase (f.)

close (v.) cerrar; closed (past tense) cerró, cerraba; (p.p. & adj.) cerrado, -a

cloth tela

clothing ropa, vestidos

cloud nube (f.)

clouded (adj.) nublado, -a

cloudy (adj.) nublado; to get cloudy nublarse

clutch (v.) coger, asir

coach coche (m.), carruaje (m.), carroza

coarse (adj.) grueso, -a

coast costa

cobbled (adj.) empedrado, -a; cobbled street calle empedrada

coffin ataúd, cajón

coin moneda

collect (v.) coger, recoger, colectar, recolectar

collection colección *(f.)*, recolección *(f.)*
college universidad, colegio
combine *(v.)* combinar
come *(v.)* venir; **came** *(past tense)* vino, venía; **come from** venir de, provenir
command *(n.)* orden, mandato, dirección; *(v.)* comandar, ordenar
comment *(n.)* comentario; *(v.)* comentar
commit *(v.)* cometer, comprometerse a; **committed** *(past tense)* cometió, cometía
communicate *(v.)* comunicar
companion compañía; compañero, -a; acompañante
compare *(v.)* comparar
compassion compasión *(f.)*
compassionate *(adj.)* compasivo, -a
compatriot compatriota *(m. & f.)*
complete *(adj.)* completo, -a; *(v.)* completar
completely *(adv.)* completamente
completion acabamiento, finalización *(f.)*, terminación *(f.)*, culminación *(f.)*
conception concepción; **Immaculate Conception** Inmaculada Concepción
confess *(v.)* confesar
confidence confidencia, confianza
confident *(adj.)* confiante *(m. & f.)*; seguro, -a de sí mismo
confront *(v.)* enfrentar, encarar, dar cara a
confuse *(v.)* confundir; **confused** *(past tense)* confundió, confundía; *(p.p. & adj.)* confundido, -a
congratulate *(v.)* felicitar, congratular(se)
conquer *(v.)* conquistar, vencer
conqueror conquistador
conquest conquista
consent consentir

consider *(v.)* considerar, tener consideración, tomar en consideración; **considering** *(pres. p.)* considerando
constant *(adj.)* constante *(m. & f.)*
construct *(v.)* construir
construction construcción
contain *(v.)* contener(se)
contempt desprecio, odio
content *(adj.)* contento, -a; satisfecho, -a
continue *(v.)* continuar
contribute *(v.)* contribuir
convent convento
conversation conversación
cook *(n.)* cocinero, -a; *(v.)* cocinar
cool *(adj.)* fresco, -a
corner esquina, rincón *(m.)*
corpse cadáver *(m.)*
correct *(adj.)* correcto, -a; *(v.)* corregir
cosmopolitan cosmopolita *(m. & f.)*
cost *(n.)* costo; *(v.)* costar
could *(past tense)* pudo, podía; *(pres. tense)* **can**
count *(n.)* cuenta, contaje; *(v.)* contar
count *(m.)* conde
countess *(f.)* condesa
country país; **countries** *(pl.)*
couple pareja, par *(m.)*
course curso
court corte *(f.)*
courteously *(adv.)* cortésmente
cousin primo, -a
cover *(n.)* cubierta, tapa; *(v.)* cubrir; **covered** *(past tense)* cubrió, cubría; *(p.p. & adj.)* cubierto, -a
cow vaca
cowardly *(adj.)* cobarde *(m. & f.)*; *(adv.)* cobardemente
coy *(adj.)* tímido, -a
craftsmanship labor artesanal, destreza artesanal
crazy *(adj.)* loco, -a

Crete Creta
cried *(past tense)* lloró, lloraba;
    gritó, gritaba; *(infinitive)* **to cry**
cries *(pl. n.)* gritos, llantos; *see* **cry**
crime crimen
cross *(n.)* cruz; *(v.)* cruzar
crow cuervo
cruelest *(superlative adj.)*
    cruelísimo, -a; el, la más cruel
cry *(n.)* llanto, grito; **cries** *(pl.)*
cry *(v.)* llorar, gritar; **cried** *(past*
    tense) lloró, lloraba; gritó, gritaba
cure *(n.)* cura; *(v.)* curar
curtain cortina
custom costumbre *(f.)*, hábito
cut *(n.)* corte; *(v.)* cortar
cut off *(v.)* cortar; *(adj.)* cortado, -a

D

dagger puñal
dance *(n.)* danza, baile; *(v.)* bailar,
    danzar
danger peligro; **dangerous** *(adj.)*
    peligroso, -a
dare *(v.)* atrever(se), osar
dark *(adj.)* oscuro, -a
darkness oscuridad *(f.)*
daughter hija
day día *(m.)*
dead *(adj.)* muerto, -a
deal (with) *(v.)* tratar de *(un*
    asunto), tratar con *(un asunto o*
    persona); **a great deal of** *(adj.)*
    mucho, -a; una gran cantidad de;
    (adv.) mucho, en gran medida,
    en gran cantidad
dear *(adj.)* caro, -a
dearly *(adv.)* caro, encarecidamente
death muerte *(f.)*
decide *(v.)* decidir
declare *(v.)* declarar
decorate *(v.)* decorar, adornar;
    decorated *(p.p. & adj.)*
    decorado, -a; adornado, -a
decree decreto

dedicate *(v.)* dedicar; **dedicated**
    (p.p. & adj.) dedicado, -a
dedication dedicación *(f.)*
deed hecho
deep *(adj.)* hondo, -a;
    profundo, -a
deeply *(adv.)* profundamente,
    hondamente
defeat *(v.)* derrotar, vencer
delicate *(adj.)* delicado, -a
delight delicia, placer *(m.)*
delightful *(adj.)* delicioso, -a;
    agradable *(m. & f.)*
deliver *(v.)* entregar
deny *(v.)* negar; **denied** *(past tense)*
    negó, negaba
descendant descendiente *(m. & f.)*
descend *(v.)* descender
describe *(v.)* describir
desert *(n.)* desierto; *(v.)* abandonar
deserve *(v.)* merecer (zc)
desire *(n.)* deseo, anhelo; *(v.)*
    desear, querer, anhelar
desk escritorio
desperate *(adj.)* desesperado, -a
despite *(prep.)* a pesar de
destiny destino
detection detección
determine *(n.)* determinar;
    determined *(adj.)* resuelto, -a;
    decidido, -a
devote *(v.)* dedicar; **devoted** *(p.p. &*
    adj.) dedicado, -a
diagonally *(adv.)* diagonalmente,
    en línea diagonal
diamond diamante *(m.)*
did *(past tense)* hizo; **didn't** (**did** +
    not) no hizo; *(infinitive)* **to do**
die *(v.)* morir
different *(adj.)* diferente *(m. & f.)*
difficult *(adj.)* difícil *(m. & f.)*
difficulty dificultad
dim *(adj.)* apagado, -a; opacado, -a;
    deslucido, -a; sin brillo
directly *(adv.)* directamente
disappear *(v.)* desaparecer

disappointed *(adj.)*
decepcionado, -a; disgustado, -a;
enfadado, -a

disarm *(v.)* desarmar; **disarmed**
(p.p. & adj.) desarmado, -a

discover *(v.)* descubrir

discovery descubrimiento

discreet *(adj.)* discreto, -a

discuss *(v.)* discutir, debatir

discussion discusión, debate

disdain *(n.)* desdén *(m.)*, desprecio

dish plato

dismiss *(v.)* despedir

display *(v.)* mostrar, exhibir,
exponer

dispute *(v.)* disputar; **disputed** *(p.p.
& adj.)* disputado, -a

distinguished *(adj.)* distinguido, -a

disturb *(v.)* turbar, perturbar,
molestar; **disturbed** *(p.p. & adj.)*
turbado, -a; perturbado, -a;
molesto, -a

do *(v.)* hacer; **don't** (**do** + **not**) no,
no + *imperative;* **does** *(3rd person
sing. of the pres. tense)* hace;
doesn't (**does** + **not**) no hace;
did *(past tense)* hizo, hacía; **didn't**
(**did** + **not**) no hizo, no hacía

dog perro

dollar dólar *(m.)*

dominate *(v.)* dominar

donkey asno

door puerta

doorway abertura de la puerta,
entrada

doubt duda

down *(prep. & adv.)* abajo

dozen docena

drag *(v.)* arrastrar(se)

draw *(v.)* dibujar, sacar; **drew**
(past tense) dibujó, dibujaba;
sacó, sacaba

drawer cajón *(m.)*, gaveta

dream *(n.)* sueño; *(v.)* soñar

dress *(n.)* vestido; *(v.)* vestir(se);
dressed *(p.p. & adj.)* vestido, -a

drew *(past tense)* dibujó, dibujaba;
(infinitive) **to draw**

drive *(v.)* conducir; **drove** *(past
tense)* condujo; **driven** *(p.p.)*
conducido

drop echar, dejar caer, caer(se);
dropped *(p.p.)*

drove *(past tense)* condujo;
(infinitive) **to drive**

drunk *(adj.)* borracho, -a; ebrio, -a

dry *(v.)* secar; *(adj.)* seco, -a

due (to) debido, -a (a)

during *(prep.)* durante

duty deber

dying *(adj.)* moribundo

E

each *(adj.)* cada; *(pron.)* cada uno,
cada una

ear oído, oreja

early *(adv.)* temprano

earn *(v.)* ganar, obtener, conseguir

easily *(adv.)* fácilmente

east este *(m. n.)*

easy *(adj.)* fácil *(m. & f.)*

eat *(v.)* comer; **ate** *(past tense)*
comió, comía; **eaten** *(p.p.)*
comido

echo eco

edge borde *(m.)*, orilla, filo

egg huevo

eighteen decimoctavo, -a

eighth octavo, -a

either *(prep.)* **either . . . or** o... o;
cualquier, -a *(de dos);* tanto uno
como otro

either *(adv.);* **not either** tampoco

elderly *(adj. & n.)* anciano, -a

element elemento

eleventh undécimo, onceavo,
onceno

else *(adj.)* otro, -a; otros, -as; *(adv.)*
de otra manera; **nothing else**
ninguna otra cosa; **somebody else**
otra persona; otro, -a

embrace *(v.)* abrazar(se)
embroider *(v.)* bordar; **embroidered**
  (p.p. & adj.) bordado, -a
embroidery *(n.)* bordado
emerge *(v.)* aparecer, emerger
emotional *(adj.)* emocional *(m. & f.)*
emperor emperador *(m.)*
empty *(adj.)* vacío, -a
encampment campamento
end *(n.)* fin *(m.)*, final *(m.)*;
  (v.) terminar, finalizar, acabar
enemy enemigo, -a
England Inglaterra
engraved *(adj.)* grabado, -a
enjoy *(v.)* disfrutar, gozar
enough *(adj.& pron.)* suficiente
  (m. & f.)
enter *(v.)* entrar
entire *(adj.)* entero, -a; todo, -a
entrance entrada
equal *(adj.)* igual *(m. & f.)*
equip *(v.)* equipar; **equipped**
  (p.p. & adj.) equipado, -a
escape *(v.)* escapar(se),
  escabullir(se)
especially *(adv.)* especialmente
even *(adv.)* incluso, aun, hasta
evening tarde, atardecer, noche,
  anochecer
event evento, suceso
eventually *(adj.)* eventualmente,
  en un momento dado, a su
  tiempo
ever *(adv.)* siempre, alguna vez;
  not . . . ever nunca
every *(adj.)* todo, -a; cada
everybody (=everyone) *(pron.)*
  todos, -as
everyone (=everybody) *(pron.)*
  todos, -as
everything *(pron.)* todo
everywhere *(adv.)* (en) todas partes
evil *(adj.)* malo, -a; diabólico, -a;
  (n.) maldad *(f.)*
exact *(adj.)* exacto, -a
exactly *(adv.)* exactamente

examine *(v.)* examinar
example ejemplo; **for example** por
  ejemplo
except (for) *(prep.)* excepto, menos
exception excepción
exceptional *(adj.)* excepcional
  (m. & f.)
exchange intercambio, cambio; **in
  exchange (for)** a cambio (de)
exclaim *(v.)* exclamar
excuse *(n.)* excusa, disculpa;
  (v.) excusar, disculpar, perdonar
exercise *(n.)* ejercicio; *(v.)* ejercitar,
  hacer ejercicio
exhausted *(adj.)* exhausto, -a;
  rendido, -a
expedition expedición
expel *(v.)* expulsar
experience experiencia
expire *(v.)* expirar
explain *(v.)* explicar
explorer explorador, -a
express *(v.)* expresar
exquisite *(adj.)* exquisito, -a
exquisiteness exquisitez *(f.)*
extraordinary *(adj.)*
  extraordinario, -a
extremely *(adv.)* extremadamente,
  extremamente
eye ojo

F

face cara, rostro
fail *(v.)* fracasar, fallar
faint *(v.)* desmayarse
fair *(adj.)* justo, -a; ecuánime
faith fe *(f.)*
faithful *(adj.)* fiel *(m. & f.)*
faithfully *(adv.)* fielmente
fall *(n.)* caída; *(v.)* caer(se); **fell**
  (past tense) cayó, caía; **fallen**
  (p.p. & adj.) caído, -a; **fall down**
  caer(se); **fall in love** enamorarse
false *(adj.)* falso, -a
fame fama

family familia
famous *(adj.)* famoso, -a
far *(adv.)* lejos; **far from** *(prep.)* lejos de
farewell despedida, adiós *(m.)*
farm hacienda, granja
farther *(adv.)* más lejos; **I can't go any farther** no puedo continuar
fascinate *(v.)* fascinar
fascinating *(adj.)* fascinante *(m. & f.)*
fast *(adj.)* rápido, -a; *(adv.)* rápido, rápidamente
fat *(adj.)* gordo, -a
fatally *(adv.)* fatalmente, mortalmente; **fatally wounded** mortalmente herido, -a
father padre
fault culpa
favorite *(adj.)* favorito, -a
fear *(n.)* temor, miedo; *(v.)* temer, tener miedo de
fearful *(adj.)* temeroso, -a; miedoso, -a
feast fiesta, celebración *(f.)*, festejo
feather pluma
feeble *(adj.)* débil *(m. & f.)*
feel *(v.)* sentir; **felt** *(past tense)* sintió, sentía; *(p.p.)* sentido
feeling *(n.)* sentimiento
feet *(pl. n.)* pies; *(sing.)* **foot**
fell *(past tense)* cayó, caía; *(infinitive)* **to fall**
fellow *(n.)* individuo, tipo; *(adj.)* que es colega
felt *(past tense)* sintió, sentía; *(infinitive)* **to feel**
feminine *(adj.)* femenino, -a
fever fiebre *(f.)*
few *(adj.)* pocos, -as; **a few** *(pron.)* unos pocos, unas pocas; unos cuantos; unas cuantas
fiancé *(m.)* novio; **fiancée** *(f.)* novia
field campo
fierce *(adj.)* feroz *(m. & f.)*, terrible

fight *(v.)* pelear, luchar; **fought** *(past tense)* peleó, luchó; *(p.p.)* peleado, luchado
figure *(n.)* figura, forma; **figure out** *(v.)* descubrir, resolver
fill *(v.)* llenar; **filled** *(p.p. & adj.)* lleno, -a; repleto, -a; pleno, -a; **fill in** llenar, rellenar; **fill out** llenar, rellenar
finally *(adv.)* finalmente, al fin, por fin
find *(v.)* encontrar, hallar; **found** *(past tense)* encontró, encontraba; *(p.p.)* encontrado
fine *(adj.)* fino, -a; bueno, -a; *(adv.)* bien; **finest** *(superlative)* finísimo, -a; el, la más fino, -a
finely *(adv.)* finamente
finger dedo *(de la mano)*
finish *(n.)* fin *(m.)*, final *(m.)*, acabado, terminación *(f.)*; *(v.)* terminar, acabar, finalizar
fire *(n.)* fuego, incendio; **catch on fire** incendiarse; **set fire** incendiar, encender
first *(adj.)* primero, -a; *(adv.)* primero, primeramente, en primer lugar
fisherman *(sing.)* pescador, -a; **fishermen** *(pl.)*
fit *(adj.)* idóneo, -a; apropiado, -a; apto, -a; en buen estado físico; **fit (in)** *(v.)* caber, tener cabida
fix *(v.)* fijar, marcar, establecer
flash resplandor *(m.)*, centelleo
flee *(v.)* huir, escapar; **fled** *(past tense)* huyó, huía; *(p.p.)* huido
flirt *(v.)* coquetear, flirtear
flirtatious *(adj.)* coqueta *(f.)*
flock *(n.)* grupo *(de personas o animales)*; *(v.)* moverse, ir en un grupo
floor suelo, piso
flour harina
flower flor *(f.)*
flutter agitación, emoción

fly *(v.)* volar
fold pliegue *(m.)*
follow *(v.)* seguir
following *(adj.)* siguiente *(m. & f.)*
food alimento, comida
fool *(adj. & pron.)* tonto, -a; loco, -a
foot pie *(m.)*; **feet** *(pl.)*
footstep paso, pisada
for *(prep.)* para, por, a; *(conj.)* porque
foreigner extranjero, -a
forest bosque *(m.)*, floresta, selva
forewarned *(adj.)* previamente
  avisado, -a; advertido, -a
forget *(v.)* olvidar; **forgot** *(past
  tense)* olvidó, olvidaba; **forgotten**
  (p.p.) olvidado
forgetfulness falta de memoria
forgive *(v.)* perdonar
forgiveness perdón *(m.)*
forgot *(past tense)* olvidó, olvidaba;
  (infinitive) **to forget**
forgotten *(p.p.)* olvidado; *(infinitive)*
  to forget
form *(n.)* forma, formulario;
  (v.) formar
formally *(adv.)* formalmente,
  oficialmente
fortunately *(adv.)* afortunadamente,
  felizmente
fortune fortuna
fought *(past tense)* peleó, luchó;
  (p.p.) peleado, luchado;
  (infinitive) **to fight**
found *(past tense)* encontró, halló;
  (p.p.) encontrado; *(infinitive)*
  to find
found *(v.)* fundar
frame *(n.)* marco; *(v.)* enmarcar,
  encuadrar
free *(adj.)* libre *(m. & f.)*; **to be free
  to go** estar libre
freedom libertad *(f.)*
French *(adj.)* francés, -esa
Frenchman, Frenchwoman *(n.)*
  francés, -esa
frequently *(adv.)* frecuentemente

friend amigo, -a
friendship amistad *(f.)*
frighten *(v.)* amedrentar, atemorizar
from *(prep.)* desde, de, a partir de;
  come from venir de, provenir
front *(n.)* frente *(m.)*; **in front of**
  frente a, enfrente de
fruit fruta
fulfill *(v.)* cumplir
full *(adj.)* lleno, -a; pleno, -a;
  repleto, -a
funny *(adj.)* divertido, -a;
  gracioso, -a
furiously *(adv.)* furiosamente
future futuro

G

gain *(v.)* ganar, obtener
gallop *(n.)* galope; **at a gallop** al
  galope, a galope; **at full gallop**
  a todo galope
gallop *(v.)* galopar; **galloped off**
  se alejó al galope
game juego, partido
garden jardín
gardener jardinero, -a
gate portal, portón, entrada
gather *(v.)* reunir, recolectar, juntar,
  colectar
gave *(past tense)* dio, daba;
  (infinitive) **to give**
gaze *(n.)* mirada, mirar *(m.)*;
  (v.) mirar
gemstone piedra preciosa
generosity generosidad *(f.)*
generous *(adj.)* generoso, -a
gentle *(adj.)* gentil, amable, suave
  (m. & f.); ligero, -a
gentleman *(sing.)* caballero;
  gentlemen *(pl.)*
German *(adj. & pron.)* alemán, -ana
gesture gesto, ademán
get *(v.)* obtener, conseguir, lograr,
  alcanzar; **got** *(past tense)* obtuvo,
  obtenía; **gotten** *(p.p.)* obtenido

gift regalo, obsequio
girl niña
give *(v.)* dar; **gave** *(past tense)* dio, daba; **given** *(p.p. & adj.)* dado, -a
give in ceder
glad *(adj.)* feliz; contento, -a
glitter *(v.)* relucir, brillar
glove guante *(m.)*
go *(v.)* ir(se); **went** *(past tense)* (se) fue; **gone** *(p.p.)* ido; **go in** entrar; **go out** salir; **go away** irse, marcharse; **go down** bajar, descender; **go off to** marcharse, irse; **go through** pasar; **go up** subir, ascender
goat cabra
God Dios
gold *(n.)* oro; *(adj.)* de oro; dorado, -a
golden *(adj.)* dorado, -a
good *(adj.)* bueno, -a
good-bye adiós; **say good-bye** decir adiós, despedirse
good-looking guapo, -a; bien parecido
gossip *(n.)* chisme *(m.)*; *(v.)* chismear
got *(past tense)* consiguió, conseguía; *(infinitive)* **to get**
grab *(v.)* coger, asir, prender, tomar; **grabbed** *(past tense)* cogió, cogía
gradually *(adv.)* gradualmente
grant *(v.)* conceder, otorgar, dar
grateful *(adj.)* agradecido, -a; grato, -a
gratitude gratitud *(f.)*
great *(adj.)* grande (gran); **a great deal of** *(adj.)* mucho, -a; una gran cantidad de; *(adv.)* mucho, en gran medida, en gran cantidad; **greater** *(comparative adj.)* más grande, mayor; **greatest** *(superlative adj.)* grandísimo, -a; el, la más grande; el, la mayor
greatly *(adv.)* grandemente, en gran medida, muy

Greek *(adj. & n.)* griego, -a
green *(adj. & n.)* verde
greet *(v.)* saludar
grew *(past tense)* creció, crecía; *(infinitive)* **to grow**
grieve *(v.)* llorar, lamentar, dolerse, sentir dolor
groom novio
ground suelo, tierra
group grupo
grow *(v.)* crecer; **grow accustomed** acostumbrarse, habituarse
guard guardia *(m.)*
guest huésped, -a; invitado, -a; convidado, -a
guide *(n.)* guía; *(v.)* guiar
guilty *(adj.)* culpable *(m. & f.)*
guitar guitarra
gypsy gitano, -a

H

habit hábito, costumbre
had *(past tense)* tuvo, tenía; *(auxiliary v.)* hubo, había; *(p.p.)* tenido; *(infinitive)* **to have**
hair cabello, pelo
half *(n.)* mitad; *(adj.)* medio, -a; *(adv.)* medio
half-naked *(adj.)* semidesnudo, -a
hand *(n.)* mano *(f.)*; **hand over** entregar
handkerchief pañuelo
handsome *(adj.)* guapo, -a; bien parecido
hang *(v.)* colgar, pender; *(past tense)* colgó, colgaba; *(p.p. & adj.)* colgado -a
happen *(v.)* pasar, ocurrir, suceder; **happen + *inf.*** hacer algo por casualidad; **who also happened to be very lazy** quien también sucedió que era muy perezosa; **it so happened that** sucedió por casualidad que

happiest *(superlative adj.)*
felicísimo, -a; muy feliz; el, la
más feliz; *(positive)* **happy**

happily *(adv.)* felizmente

happiness felicidad *(f.)*

happy *(adj.)* feliz *(m. & f.);* **happier**
(comparative adj.) más feliz;
happiest *(superlative adj.)*
felicísimo, -a; muy feliz; el, la
más feliz

hard *(adj.)* duro, -a; difícil, -a;
arduo, -a

hardly *(adv.)* apenas, difícilmente,
con dificultad

hardworking *(adj.)* trabajador, -a;
estudioso, -a; hacendoso, -a

harvest *(n.)* cosecha; *(v.)* cosechar

has *(3rd person of the pres. tense)*
tiene; *(auxiliary v.)* ha; *(infinitive)*
to have

hat sombrero

hate *(v.)* odiar

hatred *(n.)* odio

have *(v.)* tener; *(auxiliary v.)* haber;
haven't (**have + not**) no tiene;
has *(3rd person of the pres. tense)*
tiene; *(auxiliary v.)* ha; **had** *(past
tense)* tuvo, tenía; *(auxiliary v.)*
hubo, había; *(p.p.)* tenido

have to do tener que ver,
tratar de

he's (**he + is**) él es, está; (**he +
has**) él ha

head *(n.)* cabeza; **at the head of** a
la cabeza de, al frente de

head *(v.)* dirigirse

headache dolor *(m.)* de cabeza

heal *(v.)* curar(se)

health salud

healthy *(adj.)* saludable *(m. & f.);*
sano, -a

hear *(v.)* oír; **heard** *(past tense)* oyó,
oía; *(p.p.)* oído

heart corazón *(m.)*

heat *(n.)* calor *(m.);* **heat up** *(v.)*
calentar

heaven cielo

heavily *(adv.)* pesadamente,
mucho

heavy *(adj.)* pesado, -a

held *(past tense)* sostuvo, sostenía;
retuvo, retenía; arrestó, arrestaba;
(p.p.) sostenido; *(infinitive)*
to hold

helmet casco

help *(n.)* ayuda, auxilio, socorro;
(v.) ayudar, auxiliar, socorrer

her *(poss. adj.)* su, de ella

here *(adv.)* aquí, acá, en este
lugar

heroically *(adv.)* heroicamente

hers *(poss. pron.)* suyo, -a; de ella

herself *(pron.)* (ella) misma, (a) sí
misma

hesitate *(v.)* vacilar, dudar

hesitation vacilación

hide *(v.)* esconder, ocultar; **hid**
(past tense) escondió, escondía;
ocultó, ocultaba; **hidden**
(p.p. & adj.) escondido, -a;
ocultado, -a; **in hiding** oculto, -a;
escondido, -a

high *(adj.)* alto, -a; elevado, -a

high-pitched *(adj.)* agudo, -a

highly *(adv.)* altamente, muy

hiker viajero, -a; paseante
(m. & f.)

himself *(pron.)* (él) mismo, (a) sí
mismo

his *(poss. pron.)* suyo, -a; de él

history historia

hit *(v.)* golpear, dar en, acertar,
atinar; *(past tense)* golpeó,
golpeaba; *(p.p.)* golpeado

hold *(v.)* sostener, retener, arrestar;
held *(past tense)* sostuvo,
sostenía; retuvo, retenía; arrestó,
arrestaba; *(p.p.)* sostenido

holder el, la que sostiene, mantiene,
lleva, porta

home hogar *(m.),* casa

homeland patria, tierra natal

honesty honestidad *(f.)*
honor *(n.)* honor, honra;
  (v.) honrar
hope *(n.)* esperanza; *(v.)* **hope (for)**
  esperar, ansiar, anhelar
hoped-for *(adj.)* esperado, -a;
  ansiado, -a, anhelado, -a
horizontally *(adv.)* horizontalmente,
  en línea horizontal
horrified *(adj.)* horrorizado, -a
horse caballo
horseback *(adv.)* a caballo
hospitable *(adj.)* hospitalario, -a
hour hora
house casa
how *(adv. & conj.)* cómo
however *(adv.)* sin embargo
hug *(n.)* abrazo; *(v.)* abrazar; *(past tense)* abrazó, abrazaba
human *(adj.)* humano, -a
humble *(adj.)* humilde *(m. & f.);*
  sencillo, -a
humiliate *(v.)* humillar
humility humildad
hunchback *(n.)* jorobado, -a; *(adj.)*
  hunchbacked jorobado, -a
hundred cien, ciento
hung *(past tense)* colgó, colgaba;
  (p.p.) **hung;** *(pres. tense)* **hang**
hungry *(adj.)* hambriento, -a; con
  hambre; **to be hungry** tener
  hambre
hunt *(v.)* cazar
hurriedly *(adv.)* apresuradamente,
  aprisa, deprisa
hurry *(n.)* apuro, prisa; **in a hurry**
  con prisa; *(v.)* apresurarse,
  apurarse, darse prisa
hurt *(v.)* herir, lastimar; *(past tense)*
  hirió, hería; *(p.p. & adj.)*
  herido, -a; lastimado, -a
husband esposo, marido
husband-to-be novio, futuro
  esposo
hush *(v.)* silenciar, acallar, aquietar,
  callar

I

Iberian *(adj. & n.)* íbero, -a; ibero,
  -a
idealist *(n.)* idealista *(m. & f.);*
  idealistic *(adj.)* idealista
  (m. & f.)
idyllic *(adj.)* idílico, -a
if *(conj.)* si; **as if** como si
ignore *(v.)* ignorar, hacer caso
  omiso; **ignoring** *(pres. p.)*
  haciendo caso omiso
ill *(adj.)* enfermo, -a
illuminate *(v.)* iluminar, alumbrar;
  illuminated *(past tense)* iluminó,
  iluminaba; alumbró, alumbraba;
  illuminated *(p.p. & adj.)*
  iluminado, -a; alumbrado, -a
I'm (**I** + **am**) (yo) soy
image imagen *(f.)*
immaculate *(adj.)* inmaculado, -a;
  sin mancha; **Immaculate
  Conception** Inmaculada
  Concepción
immediately *(adv.)* inmediatamente
immense *(adj.)* inmenso, -a
immortalized *(p.p. & adj.)*
  inmortalizado, -a
impede *(v.)* impedir, obstruir,
  dificultar
impediment impedimento
impressed *(p.p. & adj.)*
  impresionado, -a; maravillado, -a
imprison *(v.)* encarcelar, enviar a
  prisión
in *(prep.)* en, dentro de; *(adv.)*
  adentro, dentro; **in hiding**
  oculto, -a; escondido, -a; **in the
  meanwhile** mientras tanto
including *(prep.)* incluso, inclusive,
  incluyendo
inconsolably *(adv.)*
  desconsoladamente
inconvenience inconveniente *(m.)*
incredible *(adj.)* increíble *(m. & f.)*
indeed *(adv.)* de veras, en verdad,
  ciertamente, en efecto

independent *(adj.)* independiente
(m. & f.)
indicate *(v.)* indicar
Indies, The Las Indias *(nombre dado
originalmente a América)*
industrious *(adj.)* industrioso, -a;
trabajador, -a
industry industria
infinitive infinitivo
inform *(v.)* informar
inhabitant habitante *(m.)*
innocence inocencia; **protested her
innocence** juró su inocencia
innocent inocente *(m. & f.)*
insane *(adj.)* insano, -a; demente;
desquiciado, -a; loco, -a
insect insecto
inside *(prep.)* dentro de; *(adv.)*
dentro, adentro, para adentro,
hacia adentro
insist *(v.)* insistir
inspire *(v.)* inspirar
instant instante *(m.);* **in an instant**
en un instante
instantly *(adv.)* instantáneamente,
al instante, en el acto
intent (on) *(adj.)* con la intención de
intention ánimo
interesting *(adj.)* interesante
(m. & f.)
into *(prep.)* adentro de, dentro de,
a, en
intriguing *(adj.)* que excita la
curiosidad o el interés;
misterioso, -a
invade *(v.)* invadir
investigate *(v.)* investigar
invincible *(adj.)* invencible
(m. & f.)
invite *(v.)* invitar, convidar,
participar
Irish *(adj.)* irlandés, -esa; **Irishman,
Irishwoman** *(n.)* irlandés, -esa
is *(3rd person of the pres. tense)* es;
(infinitive) **to be**
island isla

it's (**it** + **is**) es; (**it** + **was**) fue, era
its *(poss. adj.)* su, de él, de ella, de
ello
itself *(pron.)* ese, esa, eso mismo, -a;
(a) sí mismo, -a

J

jacket chaqueta, saco, americana,
terno
jai alai jai alai, pelota vasca
jail *(n.)* cárcel *(f.)*, prisión *(f.)*;
(v.) encarcelar, aprisionar
Jew *(n.)* judío, -a; **Jewish** *(adj.)*
judío, -a
jewel joya
jeweler joyero, -a
jewelry joyería, joyas
Jewish *(adj.)* judío, -a; **Jew** *(n.)*
judío, -a
job trabajo, puesto de trabajo
journey jornada, viaje *(m.)*, travesía
joy gozo, placer *(m.)*, deleite *(m.)*
judge *(n.)* juez, -eza; *(v.)* juzgar
just *(adj.)* justo, -a; *(adv.)* sólo, tan
sólo, solamente, apenas; **to have
just** *(done something)* acabar de
(hacer algo)
justice justicia

K

keep *(v.)* guardar, mantener,
quedarse uno con algo, retener;
kept *(past tense)* guardó,
guardaba; *(p.p. & adj.)*
guardado, -a
kill *(v.)* matar, asesinar, quitar la
vida a algo
kilometer kilómetro
(aproximadamente 0.62 millas)
kind *(n.)* tipo, clase; *(adj.)* amable,
gentil, cortés
kindly *(adv.)* amablemente,
gentilmente, cortésmente, con
amabilidad

kindness amabilidad *(f.)*, gentileza, cortesía
king rey
kiss *(n.)* beso; *(v.)* besar
kitchen *(n.)* cocina
knee rodilla; **on one's knees, on bended knee** de rodillas
knew *(past tense)* supo, sabía; conoció, conocía; *(pres. tense)* **know**
knight caballero
knock *(v.)* golpear, dar golpes; **knocked him off his horse** lo tiró de su caballo
know *(v.)* saber, conocer; **knew** *(past tense)* supo, sabía; conoció, conocía; *(p.p. & adj.)* **known** conocido, -a; **knowing** *(pres. p.)* sabiendo, conociendo
knowledge conocimiento, sabiduría, saber *(m.)*
known *(p.p. & adj.)* conocido, -a; **well-known** *(adj.)* muy conocido, -a

L

laborer labrador, -a; trabajador, -a
lace encaje; **lace handkerchief** pañuelo de encaje
lack *(n.)* falta, carencia; *(v.)* carecer de; no tener, faltar
lady dama, señora
lake lago
lamentation lamentación *(f.)*, queja lastimosa
lament lamento, queja, quejido, gemido
lance lanza
land tierra
language lenguaje, idioma, lengua
large *(adj.)* grande *(m. & f.)*, de gran tamaño o magnitud; **largest** *(superlative adj.)* grandísimo, -a; muy grande; el, la más grande

last *(adj.)* último, -a; final; *(pron.)* último, -a; *(v.)* durar
late *(adv.)* tarde; **later** más tarde
laugh *(n.)* risa; *(v.)* reír(se)
lavatory lavatorio, lavabo
law ley *(m.)*, leyes, abogacía, derecho
lay *(v.)* poner, depositar
lazy *(adj.)* perezoso, -a; haragán, -a; indolente *(m. & f.)*
leader caudillo, líder *(m. & f.)*
lead *(v.)* comandar, liderar, estar al frente de; **led** *(past tense)* comandó, comandaba; *(p.p. & adj.)* comandado, -a
leaf *(sing.)* hoja; **leaves** *(pl.)*
learn *(v.)* aprender, enterarse de
least; not the least ashamed sin la más mínima vergüenza
leave *(v.)* dejar, abandonar, partir, salir; **left** *(past tense)* dejó, dejaba; *(p.p. & adj.)* dejado, -a; **take leave of** despedirse de
leaves *(pl.)* hojas; **leaf** *(sing.)*
led *(past tense)* comandó, comandaba; lideró, lideraba; estuvo, estaba al frente de; *(p.p. & adj.)* comandado, -a; *(pres. tense)* **lead**
left *(past tense)* dejó, dejaba; abandonó, abandonaba; salió, salía; partió, partía; *(pres. tense)* **leave**
leg pierna
legend leyenda
less *(adj.)* menos; **less . . . than** menos… que; *(adv.)* menos
let *(v.)* permitir, dejar; **let's (let + us) go** vayamos, vamos *(imperative)*
letter carta
liberty libertad
lie *(v.)* mentir; **lied** *(past tense)* mintió, mentía; *(p.p.)* mentido

lie *(v.)* yacer; **lay** *(past tense)* yacía; **lay down** se acostaron; **lying on the cobbled street** tendido en la calle empedrada

lieutenant teniente

life *(sing.)* vida; **lives** *(pl.)*

life-saving *(adj.)* salvador, -a; salvavidas

life-threatening *(adj.)* que hace poner en riesgo la vida; **life-threatening illness** enfermedad grave

lift *(v.)* levantar

light *(n.)* luz; **light up** iluminar, alumbrar

lightning relámpago

like *(prep.)* como, así como; *(v.)* querer, gustar

limit *(n.)* límite; *(v.)* limitar

line *(n.)* línea, raya; **line up** alinear, formar fila

linen lino

lip labio

list *(n.)* lista; *(v.)* listar, enumerar

listen *(v.)* escuchar

little *(adj.)* pequeño, -a

live *(v.)* vivir

lives *(pl. n.)* vidas; *(sing.)* **life**

living quarters habitaciones, aposento

load *(n.)* carga; *(v.)* cargar

locate *(v.)* localizar, ubicar, situar; **to be located** estar situado, -a

location ubicación *(f.)*

lock *(n.)* cerradura; **lock up** encerrar, cerrar con llave

long *(adv.)* largo, -a; **longer** *(comparative adj.)* más largo, -a

look *(n.)* mirada, mirar *(m.)*; *(v.)* mirar; **look at** mirar, fijarse en

loose *(adj.)* suelto, -a; flojo, -a

lose *(v.)* perder, extraviar; **lost** *(past tense)* perdió, perdía; extravió, extraviaba; *(p.p. & adj.)* perdido, -a

lot; a lot mucho, muchas cosas; **a lot of** mucho, -a; muchos, -as

loud *(adj.)* alto, -a; fuerte *(sonido)*; estridente *(m. & f.)*

love *(n.)* amor *(m.)*; **fall in love** enamorarse; *(v.)* amar, querer, encantar, gustar mucho

lover amante *(m. & f.)*

low *(adj.)* bajo, -a; suave *(m. & f.)* *(sonido)*; *(adv.)* bajo

loyal *(adj.)* leal

loyalty lealtad *(f.)*

luck suerte *(f.)*; **as luck would have it** por esas cosas del destino

luxurious *(adj.)* lujoso, -a

lying *(pres. p.)* yaciendo; que yacía; tendido, -a; *(infinitive)* **to lie**

M

madam señora

made *(past tense)* hizo, hacía; *(p.p. & adj.)* hecho, -a; *(infinitive)* **to make**

mad *(adj.)* enfadado, -a; enojado, -a; desquiciado, -a; loco, -a

madly *(adv.)* locamente; **madly in love** perdidamente, locamente enamorado, -a

Madonna Madona (Virgen María)

magnificent *(adj.)* magnífico, -a; magnificente *(m. & f.)*

main *(adj.)* principal *(m. &. f.)*

mainly *(adv.)* principalmente, sobre todo

major *(adj.)* principal, importante, grave

make *(v.)* hacer; *(past tense)* **made** hizo, hacía; *(p.p. & adj.)* hecho, -a

male macho, varón

man *(sing.)* hombre; **men** *(pl.)*

manage *(v.)* administrar, manejar; **to manage to** lograr, conseguir cómo

mankind humanidad *(f.)*

manners modos, modales;
  well-mannered educado, -a;
  de buenos modales
many *(adj. & pron.)* muchos, -as;
  gran cantidad de
map mapa
march *(n.)* marcha; *(v.)* marchar
mark *(v.)* marcar
market mercado
marquis marqués
marquise marquesa
marriage matrimonio, casamiento,
  boda
marry *(v.)* casar(se); **married** *(past
  tense)* (se) casó, (se) casaba; *(p.p.
  & adj.)* casado, -a; **of marrying
  age** en edad de casarse
marvelous *(adj.)* maravilloso, -a
mass misa
master amo
match *(n.)* igual, par *(m.); (v.)*
  parear, emparejar, igualar
matter *(n.)* asunto, negocio, tema;
  what's the matter? ¿qué pasa?;
  (v.) tener importancia, tener
  relevancia
may *(v.)* puede (que)
mayor alcalde, -esa
meal comida, colación
mean *(v.)* significar, querer decir;
  meant *(past tense)* significó,
  significaba; *(p.p.)* significado
meaning *(n.)* significado
means *(pl. n.)* medios
meant *(past tense)* significó,
  significaba; quiso decir, quería
  decir; *(infinitive)* **to mean**
meanwhile, in the meanwhile
  mientras tanto
medical *(adj.)* médico, -a
meet *(v.)* conocer, encontrarse con,
  reunirse con; **met** *(past tense)*
  conoció, conocía; *(p.p.)*
  conocido
meeting reunión, junta,
  asamblea

member miembro
memory memoria
men *(pl. n.)* hombres, soldados;
  man *(sing.)*
mend *(v.)* remendar, reparar,
  arreglar
merchant mercader, comerciante
mercy misericordia
merry *(adj.)* contento, -a; alegre
  (m. & f.)
mesh malla
message mensaje
messenger mensajero, -a
met *(past tense)* conoció, conocía;
  (pres. tense) **meet**
mice *(pl. n.)* ratones; **mouse** *(sing.)*
middle *(n.)* medio; **in the middle
  of** en (el) medio de, a mediados
  de
might *(v.)* podría, podía; *see* **may**
milk leche
mind mente *(f.)*, pensamiento
mine *(poss. pron.)* mío, -a;
  míos, -as
minute minuto
miracle milagro
missionary misionero, -a
mistake *(n.)* error; **to make a
  mistake** cometer un error
mistreat *(v.)* maltratar
mix *(v.)* mezclar
mixture mezcla
moan *(n.)* gemido, lamento,
  quejido; *(v.)* gemir, lamentarse,
  quejarse
mockingly *(adv.)* burlonamente,
  en son de mofa
moment momento; **at that moment**
  en ese momento
money dinero
monk monje *(m.)*
month mes *(m.)*
moon luna
moonlight luz de luna
Moor *(n.)* moro, -a; **Moorish** *(adj.)*
  moro, -a; morisco, -a

more *(adj.)* más; **more . . . than** más... que; *(adv.)* más
morning hora de la mañana; **in the morning** por la mañana; **the next morning** a la mañana siguiente
most *(superlative adj.)* el, la más
mother madre, mamá
motivate *(v.)* motivar
mountain montaña
mount *(v.)* montar
mouth boca
move *(v.)* mover(se), trasladar(se)
Mr. (Mister) Sr. (Señor)
much *(adj.)* mucho, -a; *(adv.)* mucho; **very much** mucho
mud lodo, barro
Mudejar mudéjar
murder *(n.)* muerte, homicidio, asesinato; *(v.)* matar, dar muerte, asesinar
muscle músculo
museum museo
must *(v.)* deber (de)
mute *(adj.)* mudo, -a
my *(poss. adj.)* mi, mis
myself *(pron.)* (yo) mismo, -a; (a) mí mismo, -a
mysterious *(adj.)* misterioso, -a
mystery misterio

N

name *(n.)* nombre *(m.)*; *(v.)* llamar; **named** *(p.p. & adj.)* llamado, -a
napkin servilleta
narrow *(adj.)* angosto, -a; estrecho, -a
naturally *(adv.)* naturalmente
near *(prep.)* cerca de; *(adv.)* cerca; **nearest** *(superlative adj.)* el, la más cercano, -a
near *(v.)* acercarse, aproximarse
nearby *(adj.)* cercano, -a; *(adv.)* cerca
necessary *(adj.)* necesario, -a
necessity necesidad *(f.)*

need *(n.)* necesidad *(f.)*; *(v.)* necesitar, precisar; **needed** *(p.p.)* necesitado
neighbor vecino, -a
neither *(adj. & pron.)* ninguno, -a; **neither . . . nor** ni... ni; *(adv.)* tampoco
nephew sobrino
nerve nervio
nest nido
Netherlands, The Países Bajos, Holanda
never *(adv.)* nunca
nevertheless *(adv.)* no obstante, sin embargo
new *(adj.)* nuevo, -a
newly *(adv.)* recientemente; **newly married** recién casado, -a
news *(sing.)* noticia, noticias, nuevas
next *(adj. & pron.)* siguiente; próximo, -a
niece sobrina
night *(n.)* noche; **at night** de noche, a la noche, por la noche; **every night** todas las noches
nightfall anochecer
nineteenth decimonoveno, decimonono
nobility nobleza; **title of nobility** título de nobleza
nobleman *(n.)* noble; **noblemen** *(pl.)*
noise ruido
none *(pron.)* ninguno, -a
noon mediodía; **at noon** al mediodía
nor *(conj.)* ni; **neither . . . nor** ni... ni
north norte *(m.)*
northern *(adj.)* del norte; norteño, -a
nose nariz *(f.)*
not no
note *(n.)* nota; *(v.)* anotar, notar, señalar
nothing *(pron.)* nada

notice *(n.)* nota; *(v.)* notar, fijarse
notify *(v.)* notificar
notoriously *(adv.)* notoriamente
noun nombre *(m.)*, sustantivo
novel novela
now *(adv.)* ahora
nowhere *(adv.)* (en) ningún lugar
number número
nun monja

O

o'clock en punto
oak roble *(m.)*
obey *(v.)* obedecer (zc)
object objeto
observe *(v.)* observar
obtain *(v.)* obtener
occupy *(v.)* ocupar(se); **occupied**
(past tense) (se) ocupó, (se)
ocupaba; *(p.p. & adj.)*
ocupado, -a
occur *(v.)* ocurrir; **occurred** *(past
tense)* ocurrió, ocurría; *(p.p. &
adj.)* ocurrido, -a; **it occurred to
the *indiano*** se le ocurrió al
indiano
ocean océano
of *(prep.)* de, perteneciente a,
relativo a
offer *(n.)* oferta, ofrecimiento;
(v.) ofrecer (zc)
often *(adv.)* a menudo, con
frecuencia
old *(adj.)* viejo, -a; *(comparative
adj.)* **older** más viejo, -a
on *(prep.)* sobre, encima de, arriba
de; **on** + **-ing** *(v.)* al + *inf.*
once *(adv.)* una vez, cierta vez;
once again una vez más,
otra vez
only *(adv.)* sólo, solamente
onto *(prep.)*; **fell onto the street** se
cayó a la calle
open *(v.)* abrir; *(adj.)* abierto, -a
opportunity oportunidad *(f.)*

opposite *(adj.)* opuesto, -a;
contrario, -a
or *(conj.)* o; **either . . . or** o... o
order *(n.)* orden; *(v.)* ordenar, pedir
origin origen *(m.)*
orphan huérfano, -a
other *(adj. & pron.)* otro, -a
otherwise *(adv.)* de otro modo, o si
no
ounce onza
our *(poss. adj.)* nuestro, -a; **ours**
(poss. pron.) nuestro, -a
oust *(v.)* expulsar, expeler, echar
out *(adv.)* fuera, afuera
outnumber *(v.)* superar en número
outside *(prep.)* fuera de, afuera de;
(adv.) afuera, fuera
outsmart *(v.)* superar en astucia
outstanding *(adj.)* sobresaliente,
excelente
over *(prep.)* sobre, encima de, arriba
de, por encima de; **to do
something over** volver a hacer
algo; **hand over** entregar
overcast *(adj.)* nublado, -a; **to
become overcast** nublar(se)
overcome *(v.)* vencer, superar
owe *(v.)* deber algo a alguien
own *(v.)* poseer, ser dueño de
owner dueño, -a

P

paid *(past tense)* pagó, pagaba;
(p.p. & adj.) pagado, -a; *(adj.)*
pago, -a; *(infinitive)* **to pay**
paint *(v.)* pintar
painter pintor, -a
painting pintura, cuadro
pair par
palace palacio
pale *(adj.)* pálido, -a
paper papel
paralyzed *(adj.)* paralizado, -a
parapet parapeto
parchment pergamino

pardon *(n.)* perdón; *(v.)* perdonar
parents padres *(de familia)*
part parte *(f.)*
particularly *(adv.)* particularmente, en particular, sobre todo
party fiesta
pass *(n.)* pase, paso; *(v.)* pasar
passionate *(adj.)* apasionado, -a
past *(adj.)* pasado, -a; *(n.)* pasado
pastime *(n.)* pasatiempo
path sendero, camino, ruta, curso
patrol *(n.)* patrulla, ronda; *(v.)* patrullar, rondar, vigilar
pay *(v.)* pagar; **paid** *(past tense)* pagó, pagaba; *(p.p. & adj.)* pagado, -a; *(adj.)* pago, -a
peace paz *(f.)*
people *(n.)* personas, gente, pueblo
per *(prep.)* por
perched *(adj.)* posado, -a
perhaps quizás, tal vez
peril peligro
period período
permission permiso
permit *(n.)* permiso, licencia; *(v.)* permitir, dejar; **permitted** *(p.p. & adj.)* permitido, -a
person persona
Phoenician *(adj. & n.)* fenicio, -a
pick *(v.)* coger, recoger, recolectar; **pick up** coger, tomar
picture pintura, dibujo, figura
piece pedazo
pig cerdo, cochino, chancho
pin *(v.)* prender, abrochar; **pinned** *(past tense)* prendió, prendía
pirate pirata *(m.)*
place *(n.)* lugar, sitio; *(v.)* colocar, poner, depositar
plain llano, llanura; **high plains** meseta
plan *(n.)* plano; *(v.)* planear; **planned** *(past tense)* planeó, planeaba
play *(v.)* jugar, tocar *(música o un instrumento)*

please *(adv.)* por favor, si gusta; *(v.)* complacer, agradar, hacer que guste; **to please her every whim** complacerla en todos sus caprichos
pleasure placer *(m.)*
plenty of mucho, -a
pocket bolsillo
point *(n.)* punto; *(v.)* señalar; **point out** señalar, apuntar, indicar
political *(adj.)* político, -a
poor *(adj.)* pobre *(m. & f.)*
poorly *(adv.)* pobremente
port puerto
positively *(adv.)* positivamente
possess *(v.)* poseer, tener
possibility posibilidad *(f.)*
possibly *(adv.)* posiblemente
postpone *(v.)* posponer
poverty pobreza
precious *(adj.)* precioso, -a
precisely *(adv.)* precisamente, exactamente, justamente
prefer *(v.)* preferir (ie) (i)
prepare *(v.)* preparar
presence presencia
present *(n.)* regalo; *(adj.)* presente
prestigious *(adj.)* prestigioso, -a
preterite pretérito
pretty *(adj.)* bonita, linda, guapa; *(comparative)* **prettier** más bonita, más linda, más guapa; *(superlative)* **prettiest** lindísima, guapísima, la más bonita, la más guapa, la más linda
prevail *(v.)* prevalecer (zc)
previous *(adj.)* previo, -a
previously *(adv.)* previamente
price precio
pride orgullo
priest sacerdote
prince príncipe
princess princesa
prison prisión, cárcel
prisoner prisionero, -a
probably *(adv.)* probablemente

problem problema *(m.)*
proceed *(v.)* proceder
proclaim *(v.)* proclamar
produce *(v.)* producir
profusely *(adv.)* profusamente
project *(n.)* proyecto; *(v.)* proyectar
promise *(n.)* promesa; *(v.)* prometer
property propiedad *(f.)*
prophecy profecía
protect *(v.)* proteger
protest *(v.)* protestar, reclamar, defender
proud *(adj.)* orgulloso, -a; **to be proud of** estar orgulloso, -a de
proudly *(adv.)* orgullosamente, con orgullo
prove *(v.)* probar
provide *(v.)* proveer; **provide with** proveer de; **provide for** proveer a
province provincia
publish *(v.)* publicar
pull *(v.)* halar, tirar; **pull out** sacar; **he tried to pull on the tail** trató de halar de la cola
punctually *(adv.)* puntualmente
punish *(v.)* castigar
pure *(adj.)* puro, -a; castizo, -a
purpose propósito, finalidad, objeto, objetivo
purse bolsa, bolso
pursue *(v.)* perseguir, dar caza
put *(v.)* poner

Q

quality *(sing.)* cualidad, calidad *(f.)*; **qualities** *(pl.)*
quarters; living quarters habitaciones, aposento
queen reina
quickly *(adv.)* rápido, rápidamente, en seguida
quiet *(adj.)* callado, -a; silencioso, -a; **be quiet!** ¡cállate!
quite *(adv.)* bastante, algo

R

race *(n.)* raza, carrera; *(v.)* ir a la carrera, ir deprisa, jugar una carrera
rage ira
rags harapos
rain *(n.)* lluvia; *(v.)* llover
ran *(past tense)* corrió, corría; *(infinitive)* **to run**
ransom rescate *(m.)*
rapidly *(adv.)* rápido, rápidamente
rather *(adv.)* más bien, preferentemente
reach *(v.)* alcanzar (c)
read *(v.)* leer
ready *(adj.)* listo, -a; preparado, -a
reality realidad *(f.)*
realize *(v.)* darse cuenta, realizar
really *(adv.)* realmente, verdaderamente, en realidad, muy
reason *(n.)* razón; *(v.)* razonar
rebuild *(v.)* reconstruir; **rebuilt** *(past tense)* reconstruyó, reconstruía
receive *(v.)* recibir
recently *(adv.)* recientemente; **recently cut** recién cortado, -a
recognize *(v.)* reconocer
reconquer *(v.)* reconquistar
reconquest reconquista
reconstruct *(v.)* reconstruir
recover *(v.)* recuperar(se)
red *(adj.)* rojo, -a; colorado, -a; *(n.)* rojo, colorado
refer *(v.)* referir(se)
refinement refinamiento
reflection reflejo
refuse *(v.)* rehusar(se), negarse
regain *(v.)* volver a ganar, recuperar
regards saludos
reign reinado
related *(adj.)* relacionado, -a; relativo, -a
relative *(n.)* pariente *(m. & f.)*; *(adj.)* relativo, -a; relacionado, -a

release *(v.)* liberar, soltar
relief alivio
religious *(adj.)* religioso, -a
remain *(v.)* quedar(se), permanecer
remains *(n.)* restos
remember *(v.)* recordar, acordarse
de
remind *(v.)* hacer recordar
remove *(v.)* retirar, sacar, extraer
repeat *(v.)* repetir (i)
reply *(v.)* replicar, responder,
contestar; **replied** *(past tense)*
replicó, replicaba
request *(n.)* pedido, petición; *(v.)*
pedir, requerir
respect *(n.)* respeto; *(v.)* respetar
respond *(v.)* responder
response *(n.)* respuesta
rest *(n.)* resto, descanso; *(v.)*
descansar
resume *(v.)* reanudar
retire *(v.)* retirar(se)
return *(v.)* volver, regresar
reward *(n.)* recompensa; *(v.)*
recompensar
rich *(adj.)* rico, -a
richly *(adv.)* ricamente
ride *(v.)* cabalgar, viajar, andar; **rode**
(past tense) cabalgó, cabalgaba
right *(n.)* derecha; *(adj.)*
correcto, -a; bien; **to be right**
tener razón, estar en lo cierto
ring anillo; **wedding ring** alianza
risk *(n.)* riesgo; *(v.)* arriesgarse
river río
road camino, ruta
rob *(v.)* robar, hurtar
rock piedra, roca
rode *(past tense)* cabalgó, cabalgaba;
viajó, viajaba; anduvo, andaba;
(infinitive) **to ride**
rogue *(n.)* pícaro, -a
roguish *(adj.)* pícaro, -a;
picaresco, -a
Roman *(adj. & n.)* romano, -a
romantic *(adj.)* romántico, -a

roof techo, tejado
room habitación, cuarto
rosary rosario
rose rosa
round *(adj.)* redondo, -a
route ruta; **en route to** rumbo a
ruins ruinas
run *(v.)* correr; **ran** *(past tense)*
corrió, corría

S

sack *(n.)* saco, bolsa
sacred *(adj.)* sagrado, -a
sacrifice sacrificio
sad *(adj.)* triste *(m. & f.)*; **sadder**
(comparative) más triste
saddle silla *(del caballo)*
sadly *(adv.)* tristemente, con
tristeza
sadness tristeza
said *(past tense)* dijo, decía; *(p.p. &*
adj.) dicho; *(infinitive)* **to say**
sail *(n.)* vela; *(v.)* navegar
sailor *(n.)* marinero, -a; navegante
(m. & f.)
saint santo (san), -a
Saint James Santiago
salt sal; **smelling salts** sales
(aromáticas)
same *(adj. & pron.)* mismo, -a
sandal sandalia
sang *(past tense)* cantó, cantaba;
(infinitive) **to sing**
sank *(past tense)* hundió, hundía;
(infinitive) **to sink**
satisfy *(v.)* satisfacer; **satisfied** *(past*
tense) satisfizo, satisfacía; *(p.p. &*
adj.) satisfecho, -a
save *(v.)* salvar, ahorra
saw *(past tense)* vio, veía; *(infinitive)*
to see
say *(v.)* decir; *see* **said**
scene escena
school escuela
scoundrel vagabundo, pícaro, rufián

sea mar

search *(n.)* búsqueda; *(v.)* buscar

seat *(n.)* asiento; *(v.)* sentar(se)

seclusion retiro

second segundo

secretly *(adv.)* secretamente, en secreto

see *(v.)* ver; saw *(past tense)* vio, veía; seen *(p.p.)* visto

seek *(v.)* perseguir, buscar, ir en pos de; sought *(past tense)* persiguió, perseguía; *(p.p.)* perseguido

seem *(v.)* parecer; it seems to me me parece

seen *(p.p.)* visto; *(infinitive)* to see

seize *(v.)* asir, coger, prender

sell *(v.)* vender; sold *(past tense)* vendió, vendía; *(p.p.)* vendido

send *(v.)* enviar; sent *(past tense)* envió, enviaba; *(p.p. & adj.)* enviado, -a

sentence oración *(f.)*

sentinel centinela *(m.)*

separate *(adj.)* separado, -a; *(v.)* separar

series serie

serious *(adj.)* serio, -a

seriously *(adv.)* seriamente, en serio

servant sirviente *(m. & f.)*

serve *(v.)* servir

service servicio

set *(v.)* fijar, disponer, arreglar; set out (for) partir (para); set sail hacerse a la mar

several *(adj. & pron.)* varios, -as; bastantes *(m. & f.)*; muchos, -as

sew *(v.)* coser

shall *(v.) (used to express a future action)*

shame vergüenza; what a shame! ¡qué lástima!

shape *(n.)* forma, figura; *(v.)* formar, dar forma

sheep oveja, ovejas

shepherd pastor *(m.)*

shield escudo

shine *(v.)* brillar, relucir

shiny *(adj.)* brilloso, -a; reluciente *(m. & f.)*; pulido, -a

ship barco

shirt camisa

shoe zapato; shoe shop zapatería

shoemaker zapatero, -a

shop negocio, tienda; shoe shop zapatería

short *(adj.)* corto, -a; bajo, -a

shortly *(adv.)* en corto tiempo, prontamente

should *(v.)* debe, debería, debía

shout *(v.)* gritar

show *(v.)* mostrar, demostrar

shriek chillido

shrill agudo, -a; estridente *(m. & f.)*

shy *(adj.)* tímido, -a

sick *(adj.)* enfermo, -a

side lado

sign *(v.)* firmar

silence silencio

silent *(adj.)* silencioso, -a; quieto, -a; callado, -a; mudo, -a

silently *(adv.)* en silencio

silk seda

silver plata

since *(prep. & conj.)* desde; *(conj.)* porque, dado que, puesto que

sing *(v.)* cantar; sang *(past tense)* cantó, cantaba; sung *(p.p.)* cantado

single *(adj.)* soltero, -a

sir señor

sister hermana

sit *(v.)* sentar(se); sit down sentarse

situated *(p.p. & adj.)* situado, -a

skein madeja

skirmish escaramuza, refriega, riña

skirt falda

sky cielo

slab lápida, piedra

slay *(v.)* matar, dar muerte

sleep *(v.)* dormir; slept *(past tense)* durmió, dormía; *(p.p. & adj.)* dormido, -a

slight *(adj.)* ligero, -a; leve; frágil
(*m. & f.*); pequeño, -a
slowly *(adv.)* lentamente, despacio
sly *(adj.)* astuto, -a; artero, -a; sagaz
(*m. & f.*); ladino, -a
small *(adj.)* pequeño, -a
smart *(adj.)* inteligente; astuto, -a;
vivo, -a
smelling; smelling salts sales
(aromáticas)
smile *(n.)* sonrisa; *(v.)* sonreír
smooth *(adj.)* suave (*m. & f.*); liso, -a
snow nieve
so *(adv.)* tan; *(conj.)* pues, entonces,
así
soft *(adj.)* suave (*m. & f.*); bajo, -a
(*en sonido*)
sold *(past tense)* vendió, vendía;
(infinitive) **to sell**
soldier soldado
solitary *(adj.)* solitario, -a
solitude soledad
some *(adj.)* alguno, -a; algunos, -as;
(pron.) algo
someday *(adv.)* algún día, un día
someone *(pron.)* alguien
something *(pron.)* algo
sometimes *(adv.)* a veces
son hijo (varón)
son-in-law yerno
song canción (*f.*)
soon *(adv.)* pronto
sorrow pena, pesar, dolor, lástima
sorry; to be (very) sorry sentirlo
(mucho)
sought *(past tense)* persiguió,
perseguía; *(infinitive)* **to seek**
soul alma (*f.*) (el alma)
sound sonido
source fuente; **from a good source**
de buena fuente
south sur
southern *(adj.)* del sur; sureño, -a
southernmost *(adj.)* situado, -a en
la región que está más al sur
southwest sudoeste (*m.*), suroeste

souvenir suvenir (*m.*), recuerdo
space espacio
Spaniard *(n.)* español, -a
Spanish *(n.)* lengua española; *(adj.)*
español, -a; **Spanish-speaking** de
habla hispana, de habla española
speak *(v.)* hablar; **spoke** *(past tense)*
habló, hablaba; **spoken** *(p.p.)*
hablado
spear lanza
spend *(v.)* gastar, pasar *(tiempo)*;
spent *(past tense)* pasó, pasaba;
(p.p.) pasado
spider araña
spiderweb telaraña
spin *(v.)* hilar; **spun** *(past tense)*
hiló, hilaba; *(p.p.)* hilado
spirit espíritu
spoke *(past tense)* habló, hablaba;
(infinitive) **to speak**
spoken *(p.p.)* hablado; *(infinitive)*
to speak
spot mancha, sitio, lugar (*m.*)
spun *(past tense)* hiló, hilaba; *(p.p.)*
hilado; *(infinitive)* **to spin**
st. *(abbrev.)* **saint** santo (san), -a
stable *(n.)* establo; *(adj.)* estable
(*m. & f.*)
stairs escalera
stairway escalera
stand *(v.)* estar de pie, soportar,
aguantar; **stood** *(past tense)*
estuvo, estaba de pie; **stand up**
levantarse, pararse
start *(n.)* comienzo, principio;
(v.) comenzar, empezar
state positively *(v.)* aseverar,
afirmar, asegurar
statue estatua
stay *(n.)* estadía, estancia;
(v.) quedar(se), permanecer (zc)
steal *(v.)* robar, hurtar; **stole** *(past
tense)* robó, robaba; hurtó,
hurtaba; **stolen** *(p.p. & adj.)*
robado, -a; hurtado, -a
stepfather padrastro

still *(adv.)* aún, todavía

stingy *(adj.)* avaro, -a; tacaño, -a; roñoso, -a

stole *(past tense)* robó, robaba; hurtó, hurtaba; *(infinitive)* **to steal**

stolen *(p.p. & adj.)* robado, -a; hurtado, -a; *(infinitive)* **to steal**

stone piedra

stood *(past tense)* estuvo, estaba de pie; soportó, soportaba; aguantó, aguantaba; *(infinitive)* **to stand**

stop *(v.)* parar, detener(se); **stop!** ¡alto! ¡deténgase! ¡pare!

store tienda, comercio

story historia, relato, cuento, narración

strange *(adj.)* extraño, -a; raro, -a

stranger *(n.)* forastero, -a; extranjero, -a

street calle

strength fuerza

strike *(v.)* golpear, dar un golpe; **struck** *(past tense)* golpeó, golpeaba

string cuerda, cordel

strong *(adj.)* fuerte *(m. & f.)*; **stronger** *(comparative)* más fuerte

struck *(past tense)* golpeó, golpeaba; *(infinitive)* **to strike**

student estudiante *(m. & f.)*

study *(v.)* estudiar; **studied** *(past tense)* estudió, estudiaba; *(p.p.)* estudiado

sturdy *(adj.)* robusto, -a; firme *(m. & f.)*; duro, -a; resistente *(m. & f.)*

subject *(n.)* sujeto, súbdito, materia, asignatura, tema, tópico; *(v.)* sujetar, someter

subsist *(v.)* subsistir

succeed *(v.)* suceder, tener éxito

such *(adj.)* tal, tales; **such as** tal como, tales como

suddenly *(adv.)* de repente

suffer *(v.)* sufrir

suffering sufrimiento

suitor pretendiente

sun sol

sung *(p.p.)* cantado; *(infinitive)* **to sing**

sunny *(adj.)* soleado, -a; **it's sunny** hace sol

support *(n.)* apoyo, sostén; *(v.)* apoyar, sostener, mantener

supposedly *(adv.)* supuestamente

sure *(adj.)* seguro, -a

surely *(adv.)* seguramente, ciertamente

surpass *(v.)* sobrepasar, sobrepujar, superar

surprise *(n.)* sorpresa; *(v.)* sorprender, maravillar

surrender *(v.)* entregar(se)

suspect *(n.)* sospechoso, -a; *(v.)* sospechar

sustain *(v.)* sostener, mantener, sufrir

swear *(v.)* jurar; **swore** *(past tense)* juró, juraba

swiftly *(adv.)* rápidamente, velozmente

sword espada

swore *(past tense)* juró, juraba; *(infinitive)* **to swear**

syllable sílaba

T

table mesa

tail cola, rabo

take *(v.)* tomar, coger, llevar; **took** *(past tense)* tomó, tomaba; **taken** *(p.p.)* tomado; **take leave of** despedirse de; **take off** quitar(se); **take out** sacar (fuera); **take place** tener lugar, llevarse a cabo

talented *(adj.)* talentoso,-a

tale cuento, historia, relato, narración

talk *(v.)* hablar; **talked** *(past tense)* habló, hablaba; *(p.p.)* hablado

talkative *(adj.)* conversador, -a

tall *(adj.)* alto, -a; **tallest** *(superlative)* altísimo, -a; el, la más alto, -a

tarnish *(v.)* manchar

teacher maestro, -a; profesor, -a

team equipo, grupo

tear lágrima

tearfully *(adv.)* con lágrimas en los ojos; hecho, -a un mar de lágrimas

tell *(v.)* contar, narrar; **told** *(past tense)* contó, contaba; *(p.p.)* contado

tend *(v.)* cuidar

tense *(adj.)* tenso, -a; nervioso, -a

tent tienda de campaña

than *(conj.)* que; **more . . . than** más... que

thank *(v.)* agradecer; **thanks** *(n.)* gracias; **thank you** gracias

that *(adj.)* ese, -a, -o; *(conj.)* que

that's (that + is) (eso) es; **(that + has)** (eso) ha

theft robo, hurto

their *(poss. adj.)* su, sus, de ellos

themselves *(pron.)* (ellos, -as) mismos, -as; (a) sí mismos, -as

then *(adv.)* entonces, en ese tiempo, luego, después

there allí, ahí, en ese lugar; **there is** *(sing.)*, **there are** *(pl.)* hay; **there was** *(sing.)*, **there were** *(pl.)* hubo, había; **there appeared** aparecieron; **there came an invasion** se produjo una invasión

therefore *(adv.)* por eso, por ello, por esta razón

these *(adj.)* estos, -as; *(pron.)* éstos, -as; **this** *(sing.)*

thing cosa

think *(v.)* pensar; **thought** *(past tense)* pensó, pensaba; *(p.p.)* pensado

thirsty *(adj.)* sediento, -a; con sed; **to be thirsty** tener sed

this *(adj.)* este, -a; *(pron.)* éste, -a

those *(adj.)* esos, -as; *(pron.)* ésos, -as; **that** *(sing.)*

though *(conj.)* aunque, a pesar de que

thought *(past tense)* pensó, pensaba; *(p.p.)* pensado; *(infinitive)* **to think**

thousand mil

thread hilo

threw *(past tense)* arrojó, arrojaba; tiró, tiraba; echó, echaba; lanzó, lanzaba; *(infinitive)* **to throw**

throat garganta

through *(prep.)* a través de, por

throughout *(prep.)* a lo largo de, durante, durante el curso de

throw *(v.)* arrojar, tirar, echar, lanzar; **threw** *(past tense)* arrojó, arrojaba; tiró, tiraba; echó, echaba; lanzó, lanzaba; **thrown** *(p.p.)* arrojado

thunder trueno

tie *(v.)* amarrar, liar, atar

time tiempo; **on time** a tiempo

tiny *(adj.)* pequeño, -a; pequeñito, -a

tired *(adj.)* cansado, -a

title *(n.)* título; *(v.)* titular

to *(prep.)* a, en, para

today hoy, hoy en día

together *(adv.)* juntos, -as

told *(past tense)* contó, contaba; *(infinitive)* **to tell**

tomb tumba

tomorrow *(adv.)* (el día de) mañana

tongue lengua, idioma *(m.)*

tonight *(adv.)* esta noche, por la noche, de noche

too *(adv.)* también; excesivamente, demasiado

took *(past tense)* tomó, tomaba; coger, cogía; llevó, llevaba; *(infinitive)* **to take**

tooth *(sing.)* diente; **teeth** *(pl.)*

torture *(v.)* torturar

toward *(prep.)* hacia
tower torre *(f.)*
town ciudad *(f.)*, pueblo, villa
townspeople pobladores
toy juguete *(m.)*
traitor traidor
travel *(v.)* viajar
traveler viajero, -a
treason traición *(f.)*
treasure tesoro
treat *(v.)* tratar
treaty tratado
tree árbol
tribe tribu *(f.)*
tried *(past tense)* trató, trataba;
  intentó, intentaba; *(infinitive)*
  to try
trip viaje, travesía
troop tropa
trouble problema
true *(adj.)* verdadero, -a; cierto, -a
truly *(adv.)* verdaderamente, en
  verdad, de veras
trust *(n.)* confianza; *(v.)* confiar
truth verdad *(f.)*
try *(v.)* probar, intentar; **tried** *(past
  tense)* trató, trataba; intentó,
  intentaba; *(p.p.)* tratado
turban turbante *(m.)*
turn *(n.)* turno, vez; *(v.)* voltear, dar
  la vuelta; **turn back** dar la vuelta,
  volver atrás
twice *(adv.)* dos veces
twist *(v.)* torcer, doblar, encorvar
type tipo

U

ugly *(adj.)* feo, -a
ultimately *(adv.)* finalmente, por
  último
unable *(adj.)* incapaz; **to be unable
  to** no poder
unbelievable *(adj.)* increíble
  (m. & f.)
uncle tío

uncontrollably *(adv.)*
  descontroladamente
under *(prep.)* bajo, debajo de
underneath *(prep.)* bajo, debajo de
understand *(v.)* entender;
  understood *(past tense)* entendió,
  entendía; *(p.p.)* entendido
understanding *(adj.)*
  comprensivo, -a
understood *(past tense)* entendió,
  entendía; *(infinitive)* **to
  understand**
undoubtedly *(adv.)*
  indudablemente, sin duda
unexpected *(adj.)* inesperado, -a
unexpectedly *(adv.)*
  inesperadamente
unfortunately *(adv.)*
  desafortunadamente,
  infelizmente
unhappy *(adj.)* infeliz, triste
unintentionally *(adv.)* sin querer
united *(adj.)* unido, -a; unidos, -as
unjustly *(adv.)* injustamente
unrivaled *(adj.)* sin rival, sin par
until *(prep. & conj.)* hasta
unworthy *(adj.)* que no se merece
up *(prep. & adv.)* arriba, para arriba,
  hacia arriba; **up the mountain**
  montaña arriba
upholder of justice justiciero, -a
upon *(prep.)* sobre, encima de,
  arriba de; **upon** + **-ing** *(v.)* al +
  inf.
upset *(adj.)* disgustado, -a;
  enfadado, -a; turbado, -a; *(v.)*
  disgustar, enfadar, turbar
use *(n.)* uso; *(v.)* usar
useless *(adj.)* inútil
utter *(v.)* pronunciar

V

vain *(adj.)* vano, -a; **in vain** en
  vano
valiant *(adj.)* valiente *(m. & f.)*

valiantly *(adv.)* valientemente
valuable *(adj.)* valioso, -a
value valor
varied *(adj.)* variado, -a
variety variedad *(f.)*
vein vena
vengeance venganza
vertically *(adv.)* verticalmente, en
línea vertical
very *(adv.)* muy
vest chaleco
village villa
virtue virtud *(f.)*
Visigoth *(adj. & n.)* visigodo, -a
vocal cords cuerdas vocales
voice voz *(f.)*
vow voto

W

wage war pelear una guerra, librar
una guerra
wait (for) *(v.)* esperar, aguardar
walk *(v.)* caminar
wall pared *(f.)*
want *(v.)* querer, desear
war guerra
warrior guerrero, -a
was *(past tense)* fue, estuvo; era,
estaba; *(infinitive)* to be
wash *(v.)* lavar
way vía, camino, manera; **this way,
that way** de esta manera, de esa
manera, así
we've (we + have) (nosotros)
hemos
wealth riqueza
wealthy *(adj.)* rico, -a
weapon arma
wear *(v.)* vestir, llevar (puesto),
tener (puesto); **wore** *(past tense)*
vistió, vestía; **worn** *(p.p.)* vestido
weariness cansancio
weary *(adj.)* agotador, -a;
cansador, -a
weather tiempo *(meteorológico)*

weave *(v.)* tejer; **wove** *(past tense)*
tejió, tejía; **woven** *(p.p. & adj.)*
tejido, -a
web red; **spider web** telaraña
wedding boda, casamiento
week semana
weep *(v.)* llorar; **wept** *(past tense)*
lloró, lloraba; *(p.p.)* llorado
welcome *(adj.)* bienvenido, -a
well *(adv.)* bien
well-made *(adj.)* bien hecho, -a
well-mannered *(adj.)* educado,
de buenos modales
went *(past tense)* fue, iba;
(infinitive) to go
wept *(past tense)* lloró, lloraba;
(infinitive) to weep
were *(past tense)* fueron, estuvieron;
eran, estaban; *(infinitive)* to be
west oeste *(m.)*
what *(pron.)* qué
what a shame! ¡qué lástima!
what's (what + is) qué es, lo que
es; **(what + has)** qué ha, lo que
ha
whatever *(adj. & pron.)*
cualquier, -a; lo que sea
when *(adv.)* cuándo; *(conj.)* cuando
where *(adv.)* dónde; *(conj.)* donde
where are you off to adónde vas
whether *(conj.)* si
which *(adj. & pron.)* cuál, cuáles;
(pron.) (el, la, lo) cual; (los, las)
cuales
while *(conj.)* mientras (que)
whim capricho
whisper *(v.)* susurrar
white *(adj.)* blanco, -a; *(n.)* blanco
who *(pron.)* quién, quien
whole *(adj.)* entero, -a;
completo, -a; todo, -a
whom *(pron.)* (a) quién
whose *(adj.)* cuyo, -a; cuyos, -as;
(pron.) de quién; cúyo, -a;
cúyos, -as
why *(adv. & conj.)* por qué

wide *(adj.)* ancho, -a; amplio, -a; vasto, -a; extenso, -a; **widest** *(superlative)* anchísimo, -a; el, la más ancho, -a; **among the widest known characters** entre los personajes más conocidos

wife *(sing.)* esposa, mujer; **wives** *(pl.)*

wild *(adj.)* salvaje *(m. & f.)*

will *(n.)* voluntad; **good will** buena voluntad; *(v.) (used to express a future action)*

win *(v.)* ganar, vencer; **won** *(past tense)* ganó, ganaba; *(p.p.)* ganado

wind viento

window ventana

windy; it's windy hay viento

wise *(adj.)* sabio, -a

wish *(n.)* deseo, anhelo; *(v.)* desear, anhelar

with *(prep.)* con

withdraw *(v.)* retirar(se); **withdrew** *(past tense)* (se) retiró, (se) retiraba

within *(prep.)* dentro de, en

without *(prep.)* sin

witness *(n.)* testigo *(m. & f.)*; *(v.)* presenciar, ser testigo de

woman *(sing.)* mujer; **women** *(pl.)*

won *(past tense)* ganó, ganaba; venció, vencía; *(infinitive)* **to win**

woo *(v.)* cortejar

wood madera

wooden *(adj.)* de madera

woods bosque

word palabra

wore *(past tense)* vistió, vestía; *(infinitive)* **to wear**

work *(v.)* trabajar

worker trabajador, -a

workman *(sing.)* trabajador; **workmen** *(pl.)*

world mundo

worn *(p.p.)* vestido; *(infinitive)* **to wear**

worry *(v.)* preocupar(se)

worse *(comparative adj.)* peor

worth *(n.)* valor; **to be worth** valer

worthy *(adj.)* merecedor, -a

wound *(n.)* herida; *(v.)* herir

wove *(past tense)* tejió, tejía; *(infinitive)* **to weave**

woven *(p.p.)* tejido; *(infinitive)* **to weave**

wrap *(v.)* envolver

write *(v.)* escribir; **wrote** *(past tense)* escribió, escribía; **written** *(p.p. & adj.)* escrito, -a

wrong *(adj.)* errado, -a; equivocado, -a; **to be wrong** estar equivocado, -a; estar en un error

wrongly *(adv.)* erróneamente, injustamente

wrote *(past tense)* escribió, escribía; *(infinitive)* **to write**

Y

year año

yellow *(adj.)* amarillo, -a; *(n.)* amarillo

yes *(adv.)* sí

yet *(adv.)* aún (no), todavía (no); *(conj.)* sin embargo

young *(adj.)* joven; **younger** *(comparative)* más joven; **youngest** *(superlative)* jovencísimo, -a; el, la más joven

your *(poss. adj.)* tu, tus

yours *(poss. pron.)* tuyo, -a; tuyos, -as

yourself *(pron.)* (tú) mismo, -a; (a) ti mismo, -a

Vocabulario español-inglés
Spanish-English Vocabulary

All words that appear in the text are included here, except for exact or very close cognates, definite articles, some pronouns, cardinal numbers, and names of people, places, months, and days.

The following abbreviations are used:

abbrev., abbreviation
adj., adjective
adv., adverb
art., article
conj., conjunction
dim., diminutive
f., feminine
irreg., irregular
m., masculine
n., noun

obj., object
p.p., past participle
pl., plural
poss., possessive
prep., preposition
pres. p., present participle
pron., pronoun
sing., singular
v., verb

Gender is shown for all nouns, except masculine nouns that end in **-o**, feminine nouns that end in **-a**, or nouns referring to male or female beings. Irregular verbs are marked with *(irreg.)*. Stem-changing verbs have the change indicated in parentheses: **cerrar (ie), contar (ue), pedir (i)**. Verbs like **conocer** have **(zc)** in parentheses. Verbs like **construir** have **(y)** in parentheses.

A

a to, at, in, on, by
abandonar to abandon, leave
abrazar (c) to embrace
abrazo embrace
abrir to open; **abierto, -a** *(p.p. & adj.)* opened
absoluto, -a *(adj.)* absolute; **absolutamente** *(adv.)* absolutely
absorber to absorb; **absorto, -a** *(p.p. & adj.)* absorbed
abundante *(adj.)* abundant
abundar to abound
abuso abuse, misuse

acabar(se) to finish, end; **acabar de** to have just
acariciar to caress, pet; **acariciando** *(pres. p.)* petting
acción *(f.)* action
aceptar to accept
acerca de *(prep.)* concerning, about
acercarse (qu) (a) to approach
acompañar to accompany
aconsejar to advise
acordar to agree; **lo acordado** what has been agreed
acordarse (ue) (de) to remember
acostarse (ue) to go to bed, lie down

147

acostumbrarse (a) to become accustomed to

actitud *(f.)* attitude

acto act; **en el acto** instantly

acusar to accuse

adaptar to adapt

adelante *(adv.)* forward, ahead; **en adelante** from now on, henceforth

además *(adv.)* besides; **además de** *(prep.)* besides

adentro *(adv.)* inside, within

adiós good-bye

admirador, -a *(m. & f.)* admirer

admirar to admire; **admirado, -a** *(p.p. & adj.)* admired, puzzled, surprised, in awe

¿adónde? (to) where?

adornar to adorn; **adornado, -a** *(p.p. & adj.)* adorned

advertir (ie, i) to warn

afecto affection

afortunadamente fortunately

afuera *(adv.)* outside

agonía agony

agradar to please, like

agradecer (zc) to thank, be grateful for

agradecimiento gratitude

agua water

ahí there

ahora now; **ahora mismo** right now

aire *(m.)* air

al (a + el) to the, at the

al + inf. upon + -ing verb

Alá Allah

alarmar to alarm

alcalde *(m.)* mayor

alegrar(se) to make happy, be happy

alegre *(adj.)* happy, glad

alegría happiness, joy, gladness

alejar to move something away; **alejarse** to go away, move away

alemán, -ana *(adj. & n.)* German

algo something

alguno (algún), -a *(adj.)* some, any

alhaja jewel

alianza wedding ring

alimento food

alma soul, spirit

alrededor (de) around, about

alto, -a *(adj.)* high, upper; loud (of a voice); **¡alto!** stop! halt!

allí there

alumno, -a pupil, student

amable *(adj.)* kind, nice, amiable; **amablemente** *(adv.)* kindly

amar to love

amargamente *(adv.)* bitterly

amarillo, -a *(adj.)* yellow

amigo, -a friend

amistad *(f.)* friendship

amo master, owner

amor *(m.)* love

anciano, -a *(adj.)* old, aged; *(n.)* old man, old woman

ángel *(m.)* angel

angosto, -a *(adj.)* narrow

anillo ring

ánimo, -a *(n.)* spirit; intention

anoche *(adv.)* last night

ansiosamente *(adv.)* anxiously

ante *(prep.)* before, in front of, in the presence of

antes *(adv.)* first, before, previously; **antes de** *(prep.)* before; **antes (de) que** *(conj.)* before

anterior *(adj.)* previous, before

antiguo, -a *(adj.)* old, ancient

añadir to add

año year

aparecer (zc) to appear

apellido surname

apenas *(adv.)* hardly, scarcely; *(conj.)* as soon as

apóstol *(m.)* apostle, religious leader

apreciar to appreciate

aprender to learn

apresurar(se) to hurry, hurry up

aprisa *(adv.)* quickly, hurriedly

apropiado, -a *(adj.)* appropriate

apurarse to hurry
aquel, -lla, -llo, -llos, -llas *(adj.)*
  that, those (over there); **en aquel
  entonces** at that time
aquí *(adv.)* here
árabe *(adj.)* Arabic; *(n.)* Arab
araña spider
árbol *(m.)* tree
arco arch, bow
arma weapon, arm
armadura armor
armar to arm
arquitecto architect
arrastrar to pull, drag
arriba above, over, up
arrimar to move up, bring close
arrimar(se) to draw close, draw
  near
Artá village in Mallorca
arte *(m. & f.)* art, skill
artesano artisan, craftsman
artista *(m. & f.)* artist
arzobispo archbishop
asegurar to assure, ensure
asentir (ie, i) to agree
asesino, -a assassin
así *(adv.)* so, thus, in this or that
  manner
asiento seat
asistir (a) to attend
astro star, planet
astronomía astronomy
asturiano, -a Asturian
asunto matter, subject
asustar to frighten
atajo shortcut
atención *(f.)* attention, kindness;
  poner atención to pay attention
atender (ie) to wait on, take care
  of, pay attention
atónito, -a *(adj.)* amazed, astonished
atraer to attract
atrás *(adv.)* back(ward), behind
atrever(se) (a) to dare, dare to
aun *(adv.)* even
aún *(adv.)* yet, still

aunque *(conj.)* although
avanzar to advance
avaro, -a *(adj.)* greedy, miserly;
  (n.) miser
ave *(f.)* bird
aventura adventure
avisar to notify, inform, warn
¡ay! oh!, woe!
ayuda help
ayudar (a) to help
azar *(m.)* luck, fortune, destiny

B

bahía bay, harbor
bailar to dance
bajar to get down, get out, come
  down, go down to, descend
balcón *(m.)* balcony
bajo, -a *(adj.)* low, short, soft
  (of a voice)
bajo *(prep.)* under
Baleares Spanish islands in the
  Mediterranean Sea
banquete *(m.)* banquet
bañar(se) to bathe, go for a swim
barba beard
barco boat, ship
bastar to be enough, suffice
batalla battle
batallón *(m.)* battalion
Belén Bethlehem
belleza beauty
bello, -a *(adj.)* beautiful
bendecir (i, j) to bless; **¡Que Dios
  bendiga!** May God bless!
bendito, -a *(p.p. & adj.)* blessed,
  fortunate
beneficio benefit, profit
bien well, good; **está bien** (it's) all
  right
bienvenido, -a *(adj.)* welcome
blanco, -a *(adj.)* white
blandir to brandish, wield
boca mouth
boda marriage, wedding

bolsa purse, bag
bolsillo pocket
bondad *(f.)* goodness, kindness
bondadoso, -a *(adj.)* good, kind
bonito, -a *(adj.)* pretty
bordar to embroider
borracho, -a *(adj.)* drunk, *(n.)* drunkard
bosque *(m.)* woods, forest
brazo arm
brida bridle
brillante *(adj.)* brilliant, bright, shining; *(m. n.)* diamond
brillar to shine
broche *(m.)* brooch, pin
bueno (buen), -a *(adj.)* good, fine
bulto bundle
busca search
buscar (qu) to look for

C

caballero gentleman; knight
caballo horse
cabeza head; **a la cabeza de** at the head of, heading, leading
cabo end
cabra goat
cada each
caer(se) *(irreg.)* to fall, fall down
cálculo calculation, estimate
calentura fever
calor *(m.)* heat, warmth
callar(se) to be silent, keep quiet
callado, -a *(p.p. & adj.)* quiet, silent
calle *(f.)* street
cama bed
cambiar to change, exchange
cambio change, exchange; **a cambio de** in exchange for; **en cambio** on the other hand
caminante *(m. & f.)* walker, traveler
caminar to walk
camino road; **ponerse en camino** to set out

camisa shirt
campamento encampment
campana bell
campo country, field, camp; **campo de batalla** battlefield
candelero candlestick
cansado, -a *(p.p. & adj.)* tired
cansadísimo, -a *(adj.)* very tired
cansancio weariness, fatigue
cántaro jug, pitcher; **llover a cántaros** to rain bucketsful
cantidad *(f.)* amount, quantity
capa cape
capaz *(adj.)* capable
capilla chapel
capital *(f.)* capital (city)
capitán *(m.)* captain
capricho whim
cara face
cárcel *(f.)* prison, jail
carecer (zc) to lack
cargar (gu) to carry (a load)
cargado, -a (de) *(p.p. & adj.)* loaded (down) with
caricia caress
cariño affection
cariñoso, -a *(adj.)* affectionate
carpintero carpenter
casa house, home; **a casa** home
casar(se) (con) to marry
casco helmet
casi *(adv.)* almost
casita little house
castigar (gu) to punish
castellano, -a *(adj.)* Castilian
castillo castle
causa cause; **a causa de** because of
cautivo captive
cazar (c) to hunt
caudillo leader, chief
celebrar to celebrate
centenar *(m.)* one hundred
centinela *(m.)* sentinel
cerca (de) *(adv.)* near; *(prep.)* close to

cercano, -a *(adj.)* nearby, neighboring
cerdo pig
cerrar (ie) to close
cesar to cease, stop
chaleco vest
chaqueta jacket
charla conversation, chatter
charlar to chat
chico, -a *(adj.)* little; *(n.)* little boy, little girl, child, kid
chillido shriek
chisme *(m.)* gossip
choque *(m.)* shock, clash
cielo sky, heaven
ciencia science
cien, ciento *(adj.)* hundred
cierto, -a *(adj.)* certain
cimbra wooden frame for supporting an arch
cita date, appointment
ciudad *(f.)* city
clase *(f.)* kind, class, classroom
cocina kitchen
cocinero, -a cook
coche *(m.)* coach, car
cofre *(m.)* coffer, jewel box
coger (j) to take, gather, pick up
cola tail
colegio school, college
colgar (gu, ue) to hang (up)
colonización *(f.)* colonization
colocar (qu) to place, put
color *(m.)* color
colorado, -a *(adj.)* red
columna column
combinación *(f.)* combination
combinar to combine, unite
comenzar (ie, c) to begin
comer to eat
comerciante *(m.)* merchant
cometer to commit
comida food, meal
como as, like, since
¿cómo? how?, what?; **cómo no** why, of course

compañero, -a *(n.)* companion
compasión *(f.)* compassion
compasivo, -a *(adj.)* compassionate, sympathetic
compatriota *(m. & f.)* compatriot
complacer (zc) to please
complaciente *(adj.)* pleasing, kind
completo, -a *(adj.)* complete
comprar to buy; **comprarse** to buy for oneself
comprender to understand
comprensivo, -a *(adj.)* understanding
con with
conceder to grant
conde *(m.)* count
condesa countess
confundir to confound, confuse
confesar (ie) to confess
confianza trust, confidence
confiar to trust, confide
conflicto conflict
confusión *(f.)* confusion
confuso, -a *(adj.)* confused
conmover (ue) to move, affect (with emotion)
conmovido, -a *(p.p. & adj.)* moved
conocer (zc) to know, get to know
conocido, -a *(adj.)* well known
conquistador *(m.)* conqueror, conquistador
conquistar to conquer
conseguir (i) to get, achieve; **conseguirse** to get for oneself, obtain
consentir (ie, i) to consent, agree
considerar to consider
consigo with him(self), her(self), it(self), them(selves)
constante *(adj.)* constant
construcción construction
construir (y) to construct
consuelo consolation, comfort
contar (ue) to tell, count, relate
contemplar to contemplate, gaze at

contener(se) *(irreg.)* to contain oneself

contento, -a *(adj.)* happy, glad

contestación *(f.)* answer

contestar to answer

continuar to continue

contra *(prep.)* against

contribuir (y) to contribute

convento convent, monastery

conversación *(f.)* conversation

conversador, -a *(adj.)* talkative

convertir (ie, i) to convert, transform; **convertirse en** to turn into

convidado, -a *(n.)* guest

convidar to invite

corazón *(m.)* heart

correcto, -a *(adj.)* correct

correr to run

corresponder to correspond

cortar to cut

corte *(f.)* royal court

cortés *(adj.)* courteous, polite; **cortésmente** *(adv.)* courteously

cortesía courtesy, politeness

cortina curtain

corto, -a *(adj.)* short

cosa thing

cosecha crop, harvest

coser to sew

cosmopolita *(m. & f. adj.)* cosmopolitan

costa coast

costumbre *(f.)* custom, habit; **ser costumbre** to be customary

creer *(irreg.)* to believe

Creta Crete, an island belonging to Greece

criado, -a *(n.)* servant

crimen *(m.)* crime

cristiano, -a *(adj. & n.)* Christian

Cristóbal Colón Christopher Columbus

cruz *(f.)* cross

cruzar (c) to cross

cuadro painting, picture

cuadrúpedo quadruped, four-legged

cual; el cual, la cual, los cuales, las cuales which

¿cuál? which (one)?, what?

cualquier, -a any

cuando when

¿cuándo? when?

¿cuánto, -a? how much?; ¿cuántos, -as? how many?

cuarto room, bedroom

cubrir to cover

cubierto, -a *(p.p. & adj.)* covered

cuenta account; **darse cuenta (de)** to realize

cuento story, tale

cuerda string; **cuerdas vocales** vocal cords

cuerpo body

cuervo crow

cueva cave

cuidado care; **tener cuidado (con)** to be careful (with)

cuidadoso, -a *(adj.)* careful; **cuidadosamente** *(adv.)* carefully

cuidar(se) to take care, take care of

culpa blame, fault

cultura culture

cumplir (con) to carry out, accomplish, comply; **cumplir una promesa** to keep a promise; **cumplir uno con su palabra** to keep one's word; **cumplirse (un plazo)** to expire

cura *(m.)* priest

curar to cure

curioso, -a *(adj.)* curious

curso course

cuyo, -a, -os, -as whose

D

dama lady

dar *(irreg.)* to give; strike (the hour), hit; **darse cuenta (de)** to realize; **darse por vencido, -a** to yield, give up, surrender

de *(prep.)* of, off, from, with, by, about, than, away from

debajo (de) *(prep.)* under, underneath, beneath

deber *(m.)* duty; *(v.)* to have to, must, should, ought to

debido, -a *(p.p. & adj.)* due, owing; **debido a** due to

decidir to decide

decir *(irreg.)* to say, tell; **dicho** *(p.p.)* said; **diciendo** *(pres. p.)* saying; **se dice** it is said

declarar to declare

dedicar (qu) to dedicate

dedicado, -a *(p.p. & adj.)* dedicated, devoted

dedo finger

dejar to leave, let; **dejar de** to stop (doing something)

del (de + el) of the, (away) from the

delantal *(m.)* apron

delante (de) in front of, before

delicadeza delicacy, delicateness

demás *(adj.)* the rest of, other; *(pron.)* the rest, the others

dentro *(adv.)* inside, within, in; **dentro de** *(prep.)* inside (of), in, within

derrota defeat

desaparecer (zc) to disappear, vanish

desaparecido, -a *(p.p. & adj.)* disappeared, vanished

desayunar(se) to eat breakfast

descansar to rest; **descanso** *(n.)* rest

descendiente *(m. & f. n.)* descendant; *(adj.)* descending

desconsolado, -a *(adj.)* inconsolable

describir *(irreg.)* to describe

descrito, -a *(p.p. & adj.)* described

descubrir to discover, uncover

descubierto, -a *(p.p. & adj.)* discovered, uncovered

desde from, since

desdén *(m.)* disdain, contempt

desdichado, -a *(adj.)* unfortunate

desear to wish, desire

deseo wish, desire

desesperar(se) to despair

desgracia misfortune

desierto desert

desmayarse to faint

desnudo, -a *(adj.)* naked

despachar to send

despedir(se) (i) (de) to take leave of, dismiss, say good-bye to

despertar(se) (ie) to wake up

después *(adv.)* afterwards, then, later; **después de** *(prep.)* after

destacarse (qu) to distinguish oneself, to stand out

detrás *(adv.)* behind, in the back; **detrás de** *(prep.)* behind, in the back of

devoción *(f.)* devotion

devolver (ue) to return, give back

devoto, -a *(adj.)* devout

día *(m.)* day; **hoy en día** nowadays

diabólico, -a diabolic

diagonal *(adj.)* diagonal

dibujo drawing; **dibujito** little drawing

diente *(m.)* tooth

diferente different

difícil *(adj.)* difficult

dificultad *(f.)* difficulty

digno, -a *(adj.)* worthy

dinero money

Dios God

dirección *(f.)* direction, address

directo, -a *(adj.)* direct, straight

dirigir (j) to direct; **dirigirse (j) (a)** to turn to, make one's way, address (someone)

discreto, -a *(adj.)* discreet

disponer *(irreg.)* to dispose, arrange

distinguir(se) *(irreg.)* to distinguish (oneself)

distinto, -a *(adj.)* distinct, different

distraer(se) *(irreg.)* to amuse oneself, distract oneself

doble *(adj.)* double
docena dozen
doler (ue) to ache, hurt
dolor *(m.)* pain
dominar to dominate, control, tame
don *(m.);* **doña** *(f.)* titles of nobility used before a first name
doncella young woman
donde *(conj.)* where; **¿dónde?** where?; **¿adónde?** (to) where?; **¿de dónde?** (from) where?
dormir (ue) to sleep; **dormirse** to fall asleep
dormitorio bedroom
duda doubt
dueño, -a *(n.)* owner
dulce *(adj.)* sweet; *(m. n.)* candy
durante *(prep.)* during
durar to last
duro, -a *(adj.)* hard, rough, tough; **duro** *(n.)* old Spanish coin of small value

E

e and (in place of **y** before a word beginning with **i** or **hi**)
eco echo
echar to drop, throw (out)
edad *(f.)* age
edicto edict, decree
educación *(f.)* education; manners
educado, -a educated, well-mannered
efecto effect, consequence; **en efecto** indeed, as a matter of fact
ejemplo example; **por ejemplo** for example
ejército army
él *(pron.)* he, it, him
elemento element
ella *(pron.)* she, it, her
ellos, -as *(pron.)* they, them
embarcar (qu) to embark
embargo impediment; **sin embargo** nevertheless, however

emoción *(f.)* emotion
emocionado, -a *(p.p. & adj.)* excited, moved
empedrado, -a cobbled
empeorar to get worse
empezar (ie, c) to begin
en *(prep.)* in, into, on, onto, at, upon
encargar (gu) to put in charge, entrust, commission
encargado, -a *(p.p. & adj.)* entrusted, in charge
enamorarse (de) to fall in love (with)
encender (ie) to set fire to, light up; **encenderse** to catch on fire, light (up)
encerrar (ie) to lock up
encontrar (ue) to find, meet; **encontrarse** to be located; **encontrarse con** to meet, run into
encorvar to curve, bend
encorvado, -a *(p.p. & adj.)* bent, hunchbacked
enemigo, -a *(n.)* enemy
enfermar(se) to become ill
enfermo, -a *(adj.)* sick, ill
ensillar to saddle
entender (ie) to understand
enterarse (de) to learn, find out
entonces *(adv.)* then; **en aquel entonces** at that time
entrada entrance
entrar to enter, go in, come in
entre *(prep.)* among, between
entregar (gu) to deliver, hand over, surrender
entristecido, -a *(pp. & adj.)* saddened
enviar to send
envolver (ue) to wrap, envelop
envuelto, -a *(p.p. & adj.)* wrapped, enveloped
era, eran (ser) was, were
error *(m.)* error, mistake
escabullirse to escape, evade

escalera stairs, stairway
escapar(se) to escape
escena scene
esclavo, -a slave
escoger (j) to choose
escogido, -a *(p.p. & adj.)* chosen
esconder to hide; **escondido, -a** *(p.p. & adj.)* hidden
escondite *(m.)* hiding place
escribir to write; **escrito, -a** *(p.p. & adj.)* written
escuchar to listen (to)
escudo shield
ese, -a *(adj.)* that (near you); **esos, -as** those (near you)
ése, -a, -os, -as *(pron.)* that one, those (near you)
eso that (in general), that (thing); **por eso** therefore, that's why
espacio space
espada sword
espalda back; **de espaldas** with back turned
España Spain
español, -a *(adj.)* Spanish; *(n.)* Spaniard, Spanish man, Spanish woman
especial *(adj.)* special; **especialmente** *(adv.)* especially
esperanza hope
esperar to hope, wait (for), expect
espina thorn, spine
espléndido, -a *(adj.)* splendid
esplendor *(m.)* splendor
esposa wife
esposo husband
esquina corner
establo stable, barn
estar *(irreg.)* to be; **estar bien** to be well; **estar de acuerdo** to agree; **estar por** to be about to
estatua statue
este, -a *(adj.)* this; **estos, -as** these
éste, -a; -os, -as *(pron.)* this one; these
este *(m.)* east

Esteban Stephen, Steve
estimular to stimulate, excite
esto *(pron.)* this
estocada stab
estudiante *(m. & f.)* student
estudiar to study
estúpido, -a *(adj.)* stupid
examinar to examine
excelente *(adj.)* excellent
excepción *(f.)* exception
excepcional exceptional
excepto *(adv.)* except
excitar to excite
exclamar to exclaim
existir to exist
explicación *(f.)* explanation
explicar (qu) to explain
expresar to express
expresión *(f.)* expression
expulsar to expel, drive out
exquisitez *(f.)* exquisiteness
exquisito, -a *(adj.)* exquisite
extranjero, -a *(adj.)* foreign; *(n.)* foreigner, stranger
extrañar to seem strange, be surprising; to miss; **extrañarse** to be surprised, wonder
extraño, -a *(adj.)* strange
extraordinario, -a *(adj.)* extraordinary

F

fácil *(adj.)* easy; **fácilmente** *(adv.)* easily
falda skirt
falta lack
fama fame
familia family
famoso, -a *(adj.)* famous
fantástico, -a *(adj.)* fantastic
fatiga fatigue
fatigado, -a *(p.p. & adj.)* fatigued, weary
favorito, -a *(adj.)* favorite
fe *(f.)* faith

felicidad *(f.)* happiness
felicitar to congratulate; **felicitarse**
  to congratulate oneself
feliz *(adj.)* happy
fenicio, -a *(adj. & n.)* Phoenician
feo, -a *(adj.)* ugly
feria fair
Fernando Ferdinand
feroz *(adj.)* fierce, ferocious
fiarse de to trust
fiel *(adj.)* faithful; **fielmente** *(adv.)*
  faithfully
fiesta feast, festival, holiday, party
figura figure, shape
fijar to fix, set; **fijarse (en)** to notice
fijo, -a *(adj.)* fixed, set
fin *(m.)* end; **al fin, por fin** finally,
  at last; **al fin y al cabo** after all
fino, -a *(adj.)* fine, thin
firmar to sign
flecha arrow
flor *(f.)* flower
forma form, shape
formar to form
fortuna fortune, luck
francés, francesa *(adj.)* French;
  (n.) Frenchman, French woman
Francia France
frase *(f.)* phrase
fresco, -a *(adj.)* cool, fresh
fruta fruit
fuego fire
fuente *(f.)* source, fountain
fuera *(adv.)* out, outside; **fuera de**
  sí beside oneself
fuerte *(adj.)* hard, loud, strong
fuerza force, strength
fundar to found
furia fury
furioso, -a *(adj.)* furious

G

galope *(m.)* gallop; **a galope, al**
  galope at a gallop; **a todo galope**
  at full gallop

ganar to earn, gain
garganta throat
gastar to spend
generosidad *(f.)* generosity
generoso, -a *(adj.)* generous
gente *(f.)* people
geográfico, -a *(adj.)* geographic
gesto gesture
gitano, -a *(adj. & n.)* gypsy
gordo, -a *(adj.)* fat
gozar (c) (de) to enjoy
gozo pleasure
gracias thanks, thank you
granada pomegranate
grande, gran *(adj.)* large, great, big
gratitud *(f.)* gratitude
grave *(adj.)* grave, serious;
  gravemente *(adv.)* gravely,
  seriously
griego, -a *(adj. & n.)* Greek
gritar to shout
grito shout
grueso, -a *(adj.)* heavy, coarse
grupo group
gruta grotto, cave
guante *(m.)* glove
guapo, -a *(adj.)* handsome,
  good-looking
guardar to guard, keep
guerra war; **hacer (la) guerra,**
  librar una guerra to wage war
guerrero, -a *(adj.)* warring,
  bellicose; *(n.)* warrior
guía *(m. & f.)* guide, leader
guiar to guide
gustar to be pleasing, like
gusto pleasure; **con (mucho) gusto**
  with (great) pleasure, gladly

H

haber *(auxiliary v.)* *(irreg.)* to have;
  hay there is, there are; **no hay**
  como there's nothing like; **hubo**
  (preterite), **había** *(imperfect)* there
  was, there were

habilidad *(f.)* ability, skill
habitación *(f.)* room, bedroom; **habitaciones** *(pl.)* (living) quarters
habitante *(m. & f.)* inhabitant
habla speech; **de habla hispana** Spanish-speaking
hablar to speak
hacer *(irreg.)* to do, make; **hace +** ***expression of time*** (expression of time) + ago; **hecho, -a** *(p.p. & adj.)* done, made
hacia *(prep.)* toward
hacienda farm, ranch
hallar to find
hambre *(f.)* hunger; **tener hambre** to be hungry
hambriento, -a hungry, starving
harapo rag
hasta *(prep.)* until, up to; *(adv.)* even; **hasta que** *(conj.)* until
haz do (familiar command form of **hacer**)
hecho *(n.)* deed; **hecho, -a** *(p.p. & adj.)* done, made
heredero, -a heir
herida wound
herir *(ie, i)* to wound; **herido, -a** *(p.p. & adj.)* wounded
hermano brother; **hermanito** little brother
hermoso, -a *(adj.)* beautiful
hermosura beauty
hija daughter
hijo son, child; **hijos** *(pl.)* sons, children
hilar to spin
historia history, story, tale
hoja leaf
hombre *(m.)* man
honra honor
honradez *(f.)* honesty
honrar to honor
hora hour
horrorizado, -a *(adj.)* horrified
hospitalario, -a *(adj.)* hospitable

hoy *(m.)* today; **hoy en día** nowadays
huérfano, -a *(adj. & n.)* orphan
huésped *(m.)* guest
huir *(y)* to flee; **huyendo** *(pres. p.)* fleeing
humilde *(adj.)* humble
humillado, -a *(p.p. & adj.)* humiliated
humo smoke
hundir to sink, plunge

I

ibérico, -a *(adj.)* Iberian
íbero, -a *(n.)* Iberian
idealista *(m. & f. adj.)* idealistic; *(m. & f. n.)* idealist
iglesia church
igual *(adj.)* equal, same
iluminar to light, illuminate
imagen *(f.)* image
imaginación *(f.)* imagination
imaginar(se) to imagine
impedir to impede, hinder
impedimento impediment, obstacle
impresionar to impress
incendiar to set fire to; **incendiarse** to catch on fire, burn
incendio fire
inclinación *(f.)* inclination, nod
inclinar(se) to bend (over), stoop
incomodidad *(f.)* inconvenience
inconsolable *(adj.)* inconsolable; **inconsolablemente** *(adv.)* inconsolably
increíble *(adj.)* incredible
independiente *(adj.)* independent
indiano, -a *(adj.)* pertaining to the West or East Indies; *(n.)* Spaniard who returns to Spain after living in Spanish America
Indias, las Indias (The) Indies
indicación *(f.)* indication
indicar *(qu)* to indicate

indigno, -a *(adj.)* unworthy
industrioso, -a *(adj.)* industrious
inesperado, -a *(adj.)* unexpected
infeliz *(adj.)* unhappy
infinitivo infinitive
Inmaculada Concepción
  Immaculate Conception
inmediatamente *(adv.)*
  immediately
inmenso, -a *(adj.)* immense
inmóvil *(adj.)* immovable,
  motionless
insistir to insist
instante *(m.)* instant; **al instante**
  at once
inteligente *(adj.)* intelligent
intención *(f.)* intention
intentar to try, attempt
interés *(m.)* interest
interesante *(adj.)* interesting
interesar to interest; **interesarse** to
  become interested; **estar
  interesado, -a** to be interested
interiormente *(adv.)* inwardly
inútil *(adj.)* useless
invadir to invade
invitar to invite; **invitado, -a** *(p.p. &
  adj.)* invited; *(n.)* guest
ir *(irreg.)* to go; **irse** to go (away);
  fue he, she, it went; **fueron** they
  went; **iba** he, she, it was going
ira anger
Irlanda Ireland
isla island
Islas Baleares Balearic Islands

J

jabalí *(m.)* wild boar
jai alai game played by two or four
  players with a long curved basket
  strapped to the wrist and a ball
  that is caromed off a wall
jardín *(m.)* garden
jardinero gardener
jefe *(m.)* chief, leader, boss

jorobado, -a *(adj.)* hunchbacked;
  (n.) hunchback
joven *(adj.)* young; *(n.)* young man,
  woman
joya jewel
joyería jeweler's shop, jewelry
joyero jeweler
judío, -a *(adj.)* Jewish; *(n.)* Jew
juego game
juez *(m.)* judge
juguete *(m.)* toy
junto, -a *(adj.)* together; **junto a**
  (prep.) next to, near, by
jurar to swear
justicia justice
justiciero upholder of justice

K

kilómetro kilometer (about 0.62
  miles)

L

la *(f. sing. art.)* the; *(pron.)* her, it,
  you; **las** *(f. pl. art.)* the; *(pron.)*
  them, you
labio lip
labrador *(m.)* farmer
lado side
lago lake
lágrima tear
lamento lament
lanza lance
lanzar(se) to fling (oneself), throw
  (oneself)
lápida stone slab
largo, -a *(adj.)* long; **larguísimo, -a**
  (adj.) very long, longest; **a lo
  largo de** *(prep.)* along,
  throughout
lástima pity; ¡**qué lástima!** what a
  pity!
le *(sing. pron.)* (to) him, (to) her,
  (to) it, (to) you; **les** *(pl. pron.)*
  (to) them, (to) you

leal *(adj.)* loyal
leche *(f.)* milk
leer **(y)** to read
lejos *(adv.)* far, far away; **lejos de** *(prep.)* far from
lengua tongue, language
lentamente *(adv.)* slowly
levantar to raise, lift; **levantarse** to get up
ley *(f.)* law
leyenda legend
libertad *(f.)* liberty, freedom
librar to fight, wage (war)
libre *(m. & f. adj.)* free
libro book
lienzo linen cloth, canvas
ligero, -a *(adj.)* slight, light
lindo, -a *(adj.)* pretty, beautiful
lino flax
listo, -a *(adj.)* ready, smart
literatura literature
llamar to call, name; **llamarse** to be called, named
llegar **(gu)** to arrive; **al llegar** upon (on) arriving; **llegar a ser** to become
llenar **(de)** to fill (with)
lleno, -a *(adj.)* full
llevar to take, carry, wear
llorar to weep, cry
llover **(ue)** to rain; **llover a cántaros** to rain bucketsful
lluvia rain; **lluvioso, -a** *(adj.)* rainy
lo *(m. sing. pron.)* him, it, you; **los** *(m. pl. pron.)* them, you; **los** *(m. pl. art.)* the
lo que what, that which
loco, -a *(adj.)* crazy
lodo mud
lograr to achieve, obtain, be able to
lucha struggle, fight
luego *(adv.)* then, later, soon
lugar *(m.)* place
lujoso, -a *(adj.)* luxurious
luz *(f.)* light

M

madeja skein
madona Madonna (a representation of the Virgin Mary)
madre *(f.)* mother
maestro, -a *(m. & f.)* teacher, master
magnífico, -a *(adj.)* magnificent
majestad majesty; **Su Majestad** Your Majesty
mal *(m.)* evil
malo (mal), -a *(adj.)* bad, evil
malla mail, mesh
Mallorca Majorca, largest of the Balearic Islands
mallorquín Majorcan
maltratar to mistreat
mandar to send, order
manera manner, way
mano *(f.)* hand
mantequilla butter
mañana *(adv.)* tomorrow; *(n.)* morning
mar *(m.)* sea
maravilla wonder, marvel
maravilloso, -a *(adj.)* wonderful, marvelous
marcar **(qu)** to mark
marcha march; **ponerse en marcha** to set out, start to move
marchar to go, march; **marcharse** to go away, get out
marinero sailor
marqués marquis
martes *(m.)* Tuesday
más more, most
matar to kill
matrimonio marriage
mayor older, bigger, greater; **el mayor** (the) oldest, (the) biggest, (the) greatest
me *(pron.)* (to) me, (to) myself, (for) me, (for) myself
mediados; **a mediados de** in the middle part of
médico, -a *(n.)* physician, doctor

medicina medicine

medio *(n.)* means; **por medio de** by means of

medio, -a *(adj.)* half

mediodía *(m.)* noon; **al mediodía** at noon

meditación *(f.)* meditation

Mediterráneo Mediterranean Sea

mejor *(adj.)* better, best; **a lo mejor** probably; **lo mejor que uno pudo** the best one could

menos *(adj.)* less, least; *(adv.)* less; *(prep.)* except (for)

mensajero messenger

mentira lie

mercado market

merecer (zc) to deserve, merit

mes *(m.)* month

mesa table

meseta mesa, high plain

mezcla mixture

mezclar to mix

mi, mis *(poss. adj.)* my

mí me *(obj. of a prep.)*

miedo fear

miembro member

mientras (que) while, whereas, as; **mientras tanto** (in the) meanwhile

mil a thousand

milagro miracle

mío, -a, -os, -as *(poss. adj.)* my, of mine; **el mío, la mía, los míos, las mías** *(poss. pron.)* mine

mirada glance, look

mirar to look, look at

misa mass

misericordia mercy

misión *(f.)* mission

misionero, -a *(n.)* missionary

mismo, -a *(adj.)* same, self, very

misterio mystery

mitad *(f. n.)* half, middle

modo manner, way; **de otro modo** otherwise; **de todos modos** in any case, anyway

molesto, -a *(adj.)* bothered, annoyed

momento moment

moneda money, coin, currency

monje *(m.)* monk

montaña mountain; **montaña arriba** up the mountain

montar to mount

monumento monument

moreno, -a *(adj.)* brown, brunette, dark

moribundo, -a *(adj.)* dying

morir(se) (ue, u) to die

morisco, -a *(adj.)* Moorish

moro, -a *(adj.)* Moorish; *(n.)* Moor

mortal *(adj.)* fatal, mortal

mosca fly

mover(se) (ue) to move

muchacha girl, young woman

muchacho boy, young man

mucho, -a *(sing. adj.)* much; **muchísimo, -a** *(sing. adj.)* very much; **muchos, -as** *(pl. adj.)* many; **mucho** *(adv.)* much, a lot, a great deal; **lo mucho que** how much

mudo, -a *(adj. & n.)* mute

muerte *(f.)* death

muerto, -a *(p.p. & adj.)* dead, died, killed

mujer *(f.)* woman, wife

mundo world

músculo muscle

museo museum

música music

muy *(adv.)* very

N

nacer (zc) to be born

nacimiento birth

nación *(f.)* nation

nada *(indefinite pron.)* nothing; **nada** *(with a negative)* anything; **de nada** you are welcome; **para nada** (not) at all

nadie no one, nobody; **nadie** *(with a negative)* anyone, anybody
nariz *(f.)* nose
narración *(f.)* narration, story
naturalmente *(adv.)* naturally
navegar (gu) to sail
Navidad *(f.)* Christmas
necesario, -a *(adj.)* necessary
necesidad *(f.)* necessity, need
necesitar to need, be necessary
negar (ie, gu) to deny; **negarse** to refuse
negro, -a *(adj.)* black
nervio nerve
ni neither, nor, not even
niñez *(f.)* childhood
ninguno (ningún), -a *(adj.)* no, not any; *(pron.)* none, any
niña girl, child
niño boy, child
no *(adv.)* no, not
noble *(adj.)* noble, illustrious; *(m. n.)* nobleman
nobleza nobility
noche *(f.)* night, evening; **de noche** at night
nombrar to name
nombre *(m.)* name
norte *(m.)* north
nos *(pron.)* (to) us, (to) ourselves
nosotros, -as we; *(obj. of a prep.)* ourselves, us
nota note
notar to notice, note, point out
noticia *(sing.)* piece of news, *(pl.)* news
novela novel
novia *(f. n.)* girlfriend, fiancée
novio *(m. n.)* boyfriend, fiancé
nublar to cloud, darken; **nublarse** to grow cloudy; to become overcast
nuestro, -a *(adj.)* our, of ours; **el nuestro, la nuestra, los nuestros, las nuestras** *(pron.)* ours

nuevo, -a *(adj.)* new; **de nuevo** again
Nuevo Mundo New World, Western Hemisphere
numéricamente *(adv.)* numerically
nunca *(adv.)* never

O

o or
obedecer (zc) to obey
obra work; **obra maestra** masterpiece
observar to observe
ocasión *(f.)* occasion
ocupar(se) to occupy (oneself); **ocuparse de** to take care of (a matter)
ocurrir to occur
odio hatred
oficialmente *(adv.)* officially, formally
ofrecer (zc) to offer
oído (inner) ear
oír *(irreg.)* to hear
ojo eye
olvidar to forget
onza ounce
oportunidad *(f.)* opportunity
opuesto, -a *(p.p. & adj.)* opposed, opposite
orden *(f.)* order, command
ordenar to order, put in order, arrange
orgullo pride; **orgulloso, -a** *(adj.)* proud
oriental *(adj.)* oriental, eastern
origen *(m.)* origin
orilla shore, bank; edge; **a orillas de** on (a body of water)
oro gold
oscuridad *(f.)* darkness
oscuro, -a *(adj.)* dark
otoño fall, autumn
otro, -a *(adj.)* other, another; **otra vez** again

oveja sheep
oyente *(m. & f.)* hearer

P

padrastro stepfather
padre *(m. sing.)* father; priest;
  padres *(pl.)* parents, priests
pagar **(gu)** to pay
país *(m.)* country
palabra word
palacio palace
pálido, -a *(adj.)* pale
pan *(m.)* bread
panadero, -a *(n.)* baker
par *(m.)* pair, couple
para to, for, in order to, for the
  purpose of
paralizado, -a *(adj.)* paralyzed
parapeto parapet
parar to stop, raise; pararse to
  stand (up), get up
parecer **(zc)** to seem; parecerse a
  to resemble, look like
pared *(f.)* wall
pareja couple, pair
pariente *(m. & f.)* relative (of the
  family)
parte *(f.)* part
partir to leave, depart
pasado, -a *(p.p. & adj.)* past, last
pasar to pass; go through, go by,
  spend (time), happen, take
  place
pasear(se) to take a walk, stroll
paso step, pass, passage; paso
  franco free passage, let (me)
  through
pastor *(m.)* shepherd
patria native country, fatherland
patrón *(m.)* boss, master
paz *(f.)* peace
pecho chest, breast
pedazo piece
pedir **(i)** to ask (for), request
pegar **(gu)** to hit, beat

pelear to fight
peligro danger
peligroso, -a *(adj.)* dangerous
península peninsula
pensamiento thought
pequeño, -a *(adj.)* small
pera pear
perder **(ie)** to lose; perderse to get
  lost; estar perdido, -a to be lost
perdón *(m.)* pardon, excuse me
pereza laziness
perezoso, -a *(adj.)* lazy
pergamino parchment
período period (of time)
permanecer **(zc)** to remain
permiso permission
permitir to permit
pero *(conj.)* but
perseguir **(i)** to pursue, chase
persona person
personaje *(m.)* character
pertenecer **(zc)** to belong
perro dog
pesar to weigh; a pesar de in spite
  of, even though
pescador *(m.)* fisherman
petición *(f.)* petition, request
picaresco, -a *(adj.)* picaresque,
  roguish
pícaro, -a *(adj.)* roguish; *(n.)* rogue,
  rascal
pie *(m.)* foot
piedra rock
pierna leg
pieza piece
pila; nombre de pila first name
pintar to paint
pintor *(m.)* painter
pintura painting
pirata *(m.)* pirate
piratería piracy
pisada footstep
placer *(m.)* pleasure
plano *(n.)* plan
plantar to plant
plata *(n.)* silver

plato dish, plate (of food)
playa beach
plazo deadline, time limit
pleno, -a *(adj.)* full, complete
pobre *(adj.)* poor; **pobremente** *(adv.)* poorly
pobreza poverty
poco, -a *(sing. adj.)* little (in amount); **poco a poco** little by little; **pocos, -as** *(pl. adj.)* few
poder *(irreg.)* to be able to, can, may
poner *(irreg.)* to put, place; **ponerse** to put on; become; place oneself; **ponerse a** + *inf.* to begin to + *inf.*; **ponerse en camino, ponerse en marcha** to set out
por by, for, through, along, during, for the sake of; **por eso** therefore, that's why; **por supuesto** of course
¿por qué? why?
porque because
poseer to possess, have
posible *(adj.)* possible
posición *(f.)* position
precio price
precioso, -a *(adj.)* precious, valuable
precisamente *(adv.)* precisely, exactly
preferir (ie, i) to prefer
pregunta question
preguntar to ask
premiar to reward
preparar to prepare
presentar to present, introduce; **presentarse** to present oneself
preso, -a prisoner
prestar to lend
prevenido, -a *(p.p. & adj.)* warned
primero (primer), -a *(adj.)* first; **primero** *(adv.)* first
primitivo, -a *(adj.)* primitive, original

princesa princess; **princesita** little princess
principal *(adj.)* principal, main
príncipe *(m.)* prince
principio beginning; **a principios de** at the beginning of
prisa haste; **de prisa** hurriedly, quickly
prisionero, -a prisoner
probar (ue) to prove, try
proclamar to proclaim
producir (zc, j) to produce
profesor, -a *(n.)* professor
profundo, -a *(adj.)* deep, profound
prometer to promise
prominente *(adj.)* prominent
pronto *(adv.)* soon, right away; **de pronto** *(adv.)* suddenly
pronunciar to pronounce
propio, -a *(adj.)* own
proponer *(irreg.)* to propose, suggest
propósito goal, objective, end
proteger(se) (j) to protect (oneself)
provincia province
providencial *(adj.)* providential
próximo, -a *(adj.)* next, near
publicar (qu) to publish
pueblo town, people
puente *(m.)* bridge
puerco pig
puerta door, entrance
pues for, well, then, since; **pues bien** very well, well then, so
puesta de sol sunset
puntualmente *(adv.)* punctually
puñal *(m.)* dagger
puñalada stab
puro, -a *(adj.)* pure

Q

que that, which, who, whom, than; **lo que** what, that which

¡que buen viento le acompañe! may a good wind accompany you!; **¡que Dios bendiga...!** may God bless . . . !

¿qué? what?, which?; **¿para qué?** why?, for what purpose?

¡qué! what!, how!

quedar(se) to stay, remain

quejarse (de) to complain (about)

quemar(se) to burn, burn up

querer *(irreg.)* to want, wish, like, love; **querer decir** to mean

querido, -a *(adj.)* beloved, dear

quien who, whom

¿quién? who?, whom?

quitar(se) to take off, take out, take away

R

ramillete *(m.)* bunch, bouquet

rápidamente *(adv.)* rapidly, fast

rapidez *(f.)* rapidity, speed

raro, -a *(adj.)* rare, strange

rato short time, while

rayo ray, beam

raza race

razón *(f.)* reason; **tener razón** to be right

realizar (c) to carry out, fulfill

recepción *(f.)* reception

recibir to receive

recién *(adv.)* recently, newly

recio, -a *(adj.)* heavy, coarse

recobrar to recover

recoger (j) to pick up, catch

recompensar to reward

reconocer (zc) to recognize

reconquista reconquest

reconstruir (y) to reconstruct, rebuild

recordar (ue) to remember

recto, -a *(adj.)* straight

recuerdo *(n.)* remembrance, souvenir

redondo, -a *(adj.)* round

reflejo reflection

regalar to give, present as a gift

regalo gift

regla rule

regresar to return

reina queen

reinado reign, kingdom

reír (i) to laugh; **reírse de** to laugh at, laugh about

relación *(f.)* relation

relámpago flash of lightning

relampaguear to emit flashes of lightning

relampagueo lightning

religión *(f.)* religion

religioso, -a *(adj. & n.)* religious

relucir (zc) to shine

remiendos patches

repente; de repente suddenly

repetir (i) to repeat

replicar (qu) to reply

representante *(m. & f.)* representative

reprochar to reproach; **reprocharse** to reproach oneself

rescate *(m.)* ransom

resolver (ue) to resolve, solve

resuelto, -a *(p.p. & adj.)* resolved, solved

respeto respect

responder to respond, answer

respuesta response, answer, reply

resto remainder, rest

retirar(se) to withdraw, seclude oneself

reunión *(f.)* meeting, gathering, reunion

reunir(se) to gather, meet, get together

rey *(m.)* king; **Tres Reyes Magos** Three Wise Men, Three Kings

rico, -a *(adj.)* rich; **ricamente** *(adv.)* richly

riesgo risk

río river

rival *(m. & f.)* rival

robar to steal, rob
roble *(m.)* oak tree
robo *(n.)* theft, robbery
roca rock
romano, -a *(adj. & n.)* Roman
romper to break; **roto, -a** *(p.p. & adj.)* broken
ronda patrol, watch
rosa rose
rosario rosary
ruido noise, sound
ruina ruin
ruta route

S

saber *(irreg.)* to know, know how, learn
sacar (qu) to take out, take off, take away, pull out
sacrificar(se) (qu) to sacrifice (oneself)
sagrado, -a *(adj.)* sacred, holy
sal *(f.)* salt; **sales (aromáticas)** smelling salts
salir *(irreg.)* to leave, come out, go out; **sal de aquí** get out of here
salón *(m.)* large room
saltón, -a *(adj.)* protruding, bulging
salud *(f.)* health
saludar to greet
salvador, -a *(adj.)* saving; *(n.)* savior
salvar(se) to save (oneself)
sangre *(f.)* blood
sangriento, -a *(adj.)* bloody
sano, -a *(adj.)* healthy, sane
Santiago Saint James, patron saint of Spain
santo, -a *(adj.)* holy; *(n.)* saint
satisfacer *(irreg.)* to satisfy
satisfecho, -a *(p.p. & adj.)* satisfied
satánico, -a *(adj.)* satanic, diabolic
se (to) oneself, (to) one, to him, to her, to you, to them
seco, -a *(adj.)* dry, dried

secretamente *(adv.)* secretly
secreto secret
sed *(f.)* thirst; **tener sed** to be thirsty
seguida; en seguida at once, immediately
seguir (i) *(irreg.)* to follow, continue
según according to, as
segundo, -a *(adj.)* second
seguro, -a *(adj.)* sure, safe, secured
semana week
sencillo, -a *(adj.)* simple
sentar(se) (ie) to sit down
sentir (ie, i) to feel, be sorry
señor sir, Mr., gentleman; *(abbrev.)* Sr.
señora lady, Mrs., madam; *(abbrev.)* Sra.
señorita Miss, young lady; *(abbrev.)* Srta.
ser *(irreg.)* to be
serio, -a *(adj.)* serious; **muy en serio** very seriously
Serra, Junípero (1713–1784) Spanish missionary who founded missions in California
servilleta napkin
servir (i) to serve; **servir de** to serve as
severo, -a *(adj.)* severe, stern
si *(conj.)* if, whether
sí *(adv.)* yes; **sí** *(pron.)* *(obj. of a prep.)* himself, herself, itself, yourself, yourselves, themselves
siempre *(adv.)* always, forever, ever
siglo century
significar (qu) to mean, signify
siguiente *(adj.)* following, next; **al día siguiente** on the following day, the day after
sílaba syllable
silenciosamente *(adv.)* silently, quietly
sin without; **sin embargo** nevertheless, however

sincero, -a *(adj.)* sincere
sino but (on the contrary)
situación *(f.)* situation
situar to locate, place
sobre *(prep.)* on, upon, over, above, about
sobrepasar to surpass
sobresalir *(irreg.)* to excel, stand out, be outstanding
sobrina niece
sobrino nephew
socorro help
sol *(m.)* sun
solamente (=sólo) *(adv.)* only, just
soldado soldier
soledad *(f.)* solitude, loneliness
solemne *(adj.)* solemn
solitario, -a *(adj.)* solitary
solo, -a *(adj.)* alone, single
sólo (=solamente) *(adv.)* only, just
soltar (ue) to free, let go (of), loosen
solución *(f.)* solution
sonar (ue) to sound, ring
sonido sound
soñar (ue) to dream
sonrisa smile
soportar to bear, stand
sorprender to surprise;
   sorprenderse to be surprised;
   sorprendido, -a *(p.p. & adj.)* surprised, puzzled
sorpresa surprise
sospechar to suspect
sostener to support, sustain
su, sus *(poss. adj.)* his, her, your, their
suave *(adj.)* soft, smooth
subir (a) to go up, climb
suceder to happen
sucesor *(m.)* successor
suelo floor, earth, ground
suerte *(f.)* luck
suficiente *(adj.)* sufficient
sufrimiento suffering
sufrir to suffer

sujetar to control, subject, hold, restrain
sur *(m.)* south
suroeste *(m.)* southwest
suyo, -a, -os, -as his, hers, yours, theirs

T

tal *(adj.)* such; **tal vez** perhaps
talento talent
tallado (de piedras preciosas) gemstone cutting
también also, too
tampoco *(adv.)* either, neither, nor
tan so, as; **tan...como** as . . . as
tango Argentinian dance
tanto, -a *(sing. adj.)* as much, so much; *(pl. adj.)* **tantos, -as** as many, so many; *(adv.)* as much, so much
tarde *(f.)* afternoon; *(adv.)* late; **más tarde** later
te *(pron.)* (to) you, (to) yourself
tela cloth
telaraña spiderweb
temer to fear
temor *(m.)* fear
templo temple, church
temprano, -a *(adj.)* early; **temprano** *(adv.)* early
tender (ie) to stretch out
tener *(irreg.)* to have; **tener miedo** to be afraid; **tener que** to have to; **tener que ver con** to have (something) to do with
tercero, -a *(adj.)* third
terminación *(f.)* ending
terminar to finish, end
tesoro treasure
testigo *(m. &. f. n.)* witness
ti *(pron.)* *(obj. of a prep.)* you
tía aunt
tío uncle
tiempo time (period of time), weather

tienda tent, store
tiernamente *(adv.)* tenderly
tierra land
titular *(v.)* to title, entitle
título title
tocar (qu) to touch; play (music or an instrument)
todavía *(adv.)* still, yet
todo *(n.)* all, everything; **todo, -a** *(adj.)* all, every, any; **todo el mundo** everybody, everyone; **todos los días** every day
tolerante *(adj.)* tolerant
tomar to take, eat, drink
tono tone
tontería foolishness, nonsense
torcer *(irreg.)* to twist
tormenta storm
torre *(f.)* tower
torturar to torture
trabajador, -a *(adj. & n.)* worker
trabajar to work
trabajo work
tradición *(f.)* tradition
traer *(irreg.)* to bring; **trajeron** they brought
tragedia tragedy
traición *(f.)* treason
traicionar to betray
traidor, -a *(adj. & n.)* traitor
tras *(prep.)* after, behind
tratado treaty
tratar to try, treat; **tratar de** + *inf.* to try, attempt; **tratar de** to deal with (a subject)
tribu *(f.)* tribe
triste *(adj.)* sad; **tristemente** *(adv.)* sadly
tristeza sadness, sorrow
tronar (ue) to thunder
trono throne
tropa troop
tu, tus *(poss. adj.)* your
tú *(pron.)* you
tumbar to knock off, tear down
túnica tunic, robe

turbante *(m.)* turban, an Oriental head covering
turbar to disturb, distress, upset

U

ubicar to locate
último, -a *(adj.)* last; *(pron.)* last one
único, -a *(adj.)* only, unique; *(pron.)* only one; **lo único** the only thing
universidad *(f.)* university
universitario, -a *(adj.)* pertaining to a university
uno (un), -a *(sing. adj. & art.)* a, an, one; **unos, -as** *(pl.)* some, a few
urgencia urgency
usar to use
usted *(sing. pron.)* you; *(abbrev.)* Ud., Vd.
ustedes *(pl. pron.)* you; *(abbrev.)* Uds., Vds.

V

vacilar to hesitate
valer *(irreg.)* to be worth; **¡válgame Dios!** help me God!
valeroso, -a *(adj.)* brave, courageous
valiente *(adj.)* brave, valiant
valor *(m.)* value, worth, valor, courage
vano, -a *(adj.)* vain; **en vano** in vain
variedad *(f.)* variety
variado, -a *(adj.)* varied
varios, -as *(pl. adj.)* various, several
varón male
vasco, -a *(adj. & n.)* Basque; **vasco** *(n.)* Basque language
vascongado, -a *(adj.)* Basque
vecino, -a *(adj.)* neighboring; *(n.)* neighbor
vela candle

velocidad *(f.)* velocity, speed; **a toda velocidad** at full speed
vena vein
vencer (z) to defeat, beat, conquer
vendar to bandage
vender to sell
venganza vengeance
venir *(irreg.)* to come; **ven** *(familiar command)* come
ventana window
ver *(irreg.)* to see; **verse** to be seen, see each other, look
verdad *(f.)* truth
verdadero, -a *(adj.)* true, real
verde *(adj.)* green
vergüenza shame, embarrassment
vestido, -a *(adj.)* dressed; **vestido de** dressed in, as; **vestido** *(n.)* dress; **vestidos** *(pl. n.)* clothes
vestir (i) to dress, wear; **vestirse** to get dressed
vez *(f.)* time; **a la vez** at the same time; **a veces** sometimes, at times; **en vez de** instead of; **tal vez** perhaps; **una vez** once; **otra vez** again; **una y otra vez** again and again
viajar to travel
viaje *(m.)* trip, voyage
viajero, -a *(adj.)* traveling; *(n.)* traveler
víctima *(f.)* victim
vida life
viejo, -a *(adj.)* old; *(n.)* old man, old woman; **viejecillo, -a, viejecito, -a, viejito, -a** *(n.)* little old man, woman

viento wind
vigilancia vigilance
visigodo, -a *(adj. & n.)* Visigoth, one of the Germanic tribes that invaded Spain after the fall of the Roman Empire
virgen *(f.)* virgin
virtud *(f.)* virtue
visita visit
visitar to visit
viuda widow
viudo widower
vivir to live
volar (ue) to fly
voltear to turn (around)
voluntad *(f.)* will, wish, desire
volver (ue) to return; **volver a + inf.** to (do something) again; **volverse** to become, turn around; **vuelto** *(p.p.)* returned
voto vow
voz *(f.)* voice; **en voz alta** in a loud voice; **en voz baja** in a soft voice
vuelta turn, return

Y

y *(conj.)* and; **e** (in place of **y** before a word beginning with **i** or **hi**)
ya *(adv.)* already, now, yet
yerno son-in-law
yo *(pron.)* I

Z

zapatería shoe store, shoe shop
zapatero, -a shoemaker, cobbler
zapato shoe; **zapatito** little shoe